Feng Shui Form

Donna Stellhorn

Wishing you
Joy!

Donna Stellhorn

Published By ETC Publishing
Printed in the United States of America.

ETC Publishing
Reno, NV
www.etcpublishing.com

First Edition, First Printing 2006
ISBN 1-930038-19-4

Library of Congress Cataloging–in–Publication Data

Stellhorn, Donna, 1960–
  Feng shui form / Donna Stellhorn.— 1st ed.
    p. cm.
  Includes index.
  ISBN–13: 978–1–930038–19–6
  1. Feng shui. I. Title.
  BF1779.F4S798 2006
  133.3'337—dc22

                                        2005028128

Dedication

This book is dedicated to my dear friends,
Diane and Gary, Kelly and my husband Dannie.

Other Books by Donna Stellhorn

Fühl Dich wohl mit Feng Shui. *Published under the name of Donna Tokunaga. Münsingen–Bern: Fischer Media Verlag, 1996.*

Sage & Smudge: Secrets to Clearing Your Personal Space. *Reno, NV: ETC Publishing House, 1999.*

Acknowledgements

They say no one writes a book alone. Well, they are not kidding. I must thank my two editors Diane Ronngren for the hours she spent helping me turn my thoughts into sentences and Suzanne Hibbs for painstakingly checking every word, every comma, every em dash. Without the two of you there would be no book.

I want to thank Gary Dunham for his endless help putting the book together, Quenton Cowens for his wonderful illustrations, Lisa Kawski for use of the some of the interior shots on the back cover, and Lijie Zhao for her help with the Hanyu Pin Yin.

Contents

Part 2

Feng Shui Form

Introduction

Over the many years I have practiced Feng Shui I have met countless people who have asked me "Does Feng Shui really work?" Yes, it does; remarkably so! From a historical perspective it has worked for millions of people for thousands of years. How do I know it works? Well, something that doesn't work won't last very long. Feng Shui has been around for more than 4,000 years and been a tool for improving the lives of the people who have accessed its power during all of that time. It has worked for me personally and for the hundreds of friends, and the thousands of clients and students I have helped over the past sixteen years. My goal in writing this book is to help you learn to use the power of Feng Shui to make a real difference in your own life.

The reason Feng Shui works is because we all have a basic need to experience harmony in our environment, and we all make every effort to cause that to happen. No matter what occurs out in the world, we need a soft nest to come home to. We all need our personal space—surroundings that feel comfortable and welcoming when we get home after a long day spent in the stressful and challenging world; a special retreat from the environments of our cities, our commutes, our workplaces and the people and situations we encounter in the outside world every day. When we enjoy harmony in some physical place in our lives, we can give our full energy and attention to the people who are important to us, to our work and the things that are valuable to us on an individual, internal level. We need to feel that we have a sanctuary at home in order to live our best lives.

How much more effective do you feel at work when you enjoy a night of restful sleep? Wouldn't it be wonderful to sleep well every single night? How good would it feel to rise rested in the morning, with plenty of time and energy to exercise, complete your morning preparations and get ready for your day at a gentle, easy pace? How much more confident would you both feel and appear to others if you knew you had a welcoming home environment—one that was comfortable and beautiful and one to which you knew you could invite people at a moment's notice? How good would it feel to never again need to dash around in a panic clearing clutter and cleaning frantically when you learned that someone was coming to visit?

How much closer might you feel in your relationship with your significant other if you shared a harmonious environment to prepare meals together, if you could relax after a busy day and enjoy one another's company as you stand in the kitchen watching the meal simmer on the stove, laughing and joking with the person you love? How much more support and encouragement could you offer your children if you had space where the family could gather to share a meal or interact with one another, a calm and peaceful place (and a special time of the day) where family members had a chance to talk about their days, to share stories or make plans for tomorrow?

How much healthier would you feel if you had somewhere in your home that accommodated your needs to release the tension and stress of the day, somewhere you could stretch your muscles and limbs, a place to work out, to dance or just meditate and enjoy some quiet time? How much more peaceful would you feel if you had a place of your own to sit, to just relax and absorb a sense of peaceful quiet, perhaps with a good book on your lap, a pet sleeping nearby and some music playing softly in the background?

Feng Shui is very effective at creating the type of environment that can help you thrive and prosper. It provides guidelines and suggestions for creating just the type of safe and comfortable space you can call home. My guess is that your current dwelling is somewhere along the road to becoming your home. It will take a little effort over a short period of time to create that real feeling of the perfect home for you and those you love, but the rewards are huge. So, let's roll up our sleeves and get to work.

My wish is that you will enjoy your own Feng Shui process as much as I do mine, and every bit as much as my clients and students enjoy theirs.

Donna Stellhorn

Part 1

Chapter 1

Feng Shui Basics

What is Feng Shui?

Do you consider yourself a lucky person? In the ancient cultures of the East and West, and even to those of us living in most parts of the world today, the concept of "good luck" is a somewhat nebulous one; it can mean many things. It may mean that you are successful with your financial investments or that you win when you take a gamble. In a broad sense, it probably means that you are a "winner." To most of us it means having good fortune, dear friends, a loving spouse, successful children, an abundant source of income, a pleasant home in a nice neighborhood, good health and pleasant relationships with other members of our extended family, within our communities and with our co–workers— anything and everything that supports a good and happy life. We all know people who simply seem to have been "born lucky." Some are born into rich families, some are born beautiful, some are born with physical grace, talent or an aptitude for sports; some are born with a powerful intellect, the ability to reason and arrive at brilliant conclusions—to conceptualize, visualize, create. These are the lucky ones and things come to them easily because of their luck.

In the ancient cultures of the East, great thinkers observed that some people seemed to enjoy more "good luck" than others and posed the questions, "Why leave luck to chance?" and "How can we improve our luck?" They realized there was a kind of connection between all living things, and therefore studied the natural environment all around looking for answers to their questions. They observed that if a seed had the "luck" to fall on fertile soil, in a sunny area, nurtured by fresh water and protected from high winds, it would prosper. It seemed reasonable for them to extrapolate that if their ancestors were "planted" in the right environment, good luck would accrue to the living family members. Their next thought was, "Why not 'plant' our own homes in the best possible surroundings, in the luckiest of places and thus bring good luck into our own lives?"

The Eastern art of Feng Shui is all about finding or creating the best possible physical environment as a basis for changing and improving your luck.

For the past several thousand years the Chinese have been studying how to harmonize with the environment for the greater benefit of all. They began by determining the "best" sites to bury their deceased ancestors. For thousands of years the Chinese believed that their ancestors watched over them from the great beyond. When the ancestors approved of what their offspring were doing, they sent blessings of prosperity to the family and opportunities for great benefit in all areas of life. If the ancestors did not approve of their descendants' actions, or worse, if they were forgotten by the younger generations, the Chinese believed that the whole family was doomed to suffer all manner of ill fortune—everything from bad luck, poor health, loss of position and status in the community, to social, familial and financial disaster. It has been some years since the modern Chinese people followed all of these beliefs to such an extent, but obviously a culture based on a set of beliefs changes very, very slowly. So, many of the behaviors that became custom as a result of this way of thinking remain in the present–day culture.

As a result of this traditional way of thinking, a broad–based belief structure developed concerning the importance of choosing the best burial sites for loved ones. A whole profession grew up around the need to identify the right place to bury a loved one. At about the same time that traditional spiritual leaders began to focus on this issue, other thinkers in the region were beginning to explore and gain insight into nature and the cycles of all living things. All of this started taking place in China 4,000 to 6,000 years ago, many, many years before we in the West were even close to considering this type of question.

These ancient Chinese thinkers were the forerunners of our modern–day scientists. They observed that when seeds were planted in a place where they received abundant sunshine, fresh water and shelter from high winds, plants prospered and grew strong. Over generations, this understanding of the processes of nature was incorporated into what other thinkers and leaders were learning about identifying ideal burial sites; with ideal burial sites came prosperity to the families. As a result, communities came together to build temples in the more settled areas of the country. The temples prospered. Then, using these same basic rules based on their years of observations—concerning the way things work—communities built palaces for their rulers. Eventually homes and businesses were built based on these principles and everyone benefited. For the past 4,000 years the Chinese have been perfecting a system of rules concerning the placement of all things in order to ensure the best possible lucky outcome.

The Chinese call this entire system of thought "Feng Shui." Literally translated, Feng Shui is a compilation of the concepts inherent in the Chinese characters or symbols for wind and water. Feng Shui is a reference to heaven (where wind lives) and to the earth (where water lives). Mankind lives between heaven and earth; between wind and water. The two elements, wind and water, are the only two of the five Chinese elements that move; they flow and surge. The Chinese learned early on that it is easier to change the direction of something that is already in motion, than it is to try to move something that is standing still.

Pronunciation guide: *Feng Shui* is actually pronounced "foong shway". The commonly used English spelling is from the Hanyu Pinyin romanized system of the People's Republic of China. This system replaced previous systems after the Chinese Communist Party came into power in 1949. "Pinyin" (as it is often called) does not offer a conventional English pronunciation for the Chinese vocabulary, but it does provide a consistent spelling system. With practice we "Westerners" can learn how to pronounce the spellings we see. Another word that is often used in the context of Feng Shui books is *Qi*. You may see this word spelled: ch'i, chi, ji or, the way it is in this book, *Qi*. In every instance it is pronounced "chee."

What is Qi?

The concept of *Qi* is at the heart of Feng Shui. *Qi* is the life force, energy field or simply "the energy" that exists in all things. It is in the earth, the mountains and the rivers. It is in cities, towns and villages. It circulates in our homes and businesses as well as in our bodies. *Qi* is in everything and everybody.

Qi energy, the balance between Yin (feminine, yielding energy) and Yang (masculine, penetrating force) energies, winds its way like a river through life. Sometimes this energy moves quickly and is strong. Strong *Qi* creates mountains, forests and prosperous cities. Sometimes the *Qi* is weak, diluted and wandering. This gentler form of *Qi* creates valleys and deserts and can diminish the energy of business and prosperity. The purpose of using Feng Shui techniques is to learn how to locate existing *Qi*, to find ways of attracting it to where we want it to be, to wait observantly as we allow it to pool or build strength, and only then to reap the benefits of the collection of good *Qi* (sheng *Qi*). In Feng Shui we are also aware of bad *Qi* (sha *Qi*) and how it can affect our health, relationships and wealth. By finding the *Qi*, determining its quality and adding to the quantity of good *Qi*, we can effect great change in our lives.

Feng Shui combines the forces of Yin and Yang. There are a variety of techniques we can practice to bring these two opposing energies into balance in order to create a positive flow of *Qi*. Ideally, the combined Yin and Yang energy force flows through everything. *Qi*, which contains elements of both the Yin and Yang energies, flows like a river, like a stream of life and power through all things.

If you are a computer whiz, you might think of *Qi* as if it were a network connection—specifically a wireless network. Hitting a dead spot means no signal; hitting a dead spot in a home can mean no *Qi*. If you work in a factory you expect the conveyer belt to move the items being assembled from one part of the process to another. If the conveyer belt stops everything stands still. This is an example of *Qi* in motion in the factory. If you work in an office, think of *Qi* as you think of the paper flow moving through the business. Orders come in, copies are sent to shipping, accounting and customer service, etc. This paper flow represents the concept of the flow of *Qi*. When everything (including *Qi*) moves smoothly, the business prospers, and the benefits flow to all of the employees. When there are problems—when *Qi* energy is blocked—everything comes to a standstill.

Every action, anything you do in life, is dependent on a flow of *Qi*. When *Qi* stops flowing, everything that makes life worth living comes to a stop! However, we all need to be aware of the fact that even with *Qi*, there is a natural ebb and flow to the process of living life. There are times when things move forward, times when things slow down; there are turns and changes in direction, much like the waves of the ocean roll in and out along a sandy beach or the way a river flows more strongly as a result of a spring thaw than it might in the middle of summer. This imagery can be applied to *Qi* itself as we think about the flow of energy and of a life in process.

Different Schools of Feng Shui

It is likely that if you are holding this book, you have previously read a few Feng Shui books and are already starting to get confused. Well, I have good news, it's not you—it's the books. There is more than one system of Feng Shui. There are in fact two basic systems of Feng Shui used in China and as many as eight taught here in the United States. Although each system is valid, they are difficult to combine. To use an analogy, in the martial arts there is the fast–moving, high–kicking art of kung fu and the slow, graceful dance of Tai Chi. Both are great systems of exercise and self defense—but if you try to combine the different techniques in one move, you are going to pull a muscle. It is the same with Feng Shui. For instance, should you try to combine the traditional compass system with the ba–gua compass you will end up not knowing if you are looking "north" or "left," or at your "career." If you find information in another book that conflicts with what you learn in this book, chances are good that the other book is based on a different system of Feng Shui. Do not despair, try anything you like—just be careful not to pull a muscle.

There are several excellent systems of Feng Shui (called schools) relied upon by modern–day Feng Shui practitioners, masters, experts, teachers and students of this ancient art. Gifted and skilled practitioners of most schools can be found in many countries now (both in the East and in the West). They offer their services to the benefit of their families, students, clients and communities all around the globe.

Form School Feng Shui

Throughout this book we are going to concentrate on one system of Feng Shui, the Form School. Form School Feng Shui is

Lo-Pan Compass

Fig. 1: The *lo-pan* is the traditional compass and a tool for measuring energy. The circular piece, called heaven, rotates in the square base, called earth; at the center is a compass. Two red strings attached to the square piece quarter the round piece. These red strings draw lines across the characters that describe the energy.

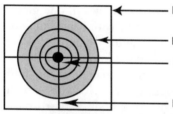

Earth: square base of the compass

Heaven: round wheel of information

Well of Heaven: the compass itself

Red String: for reading the energy

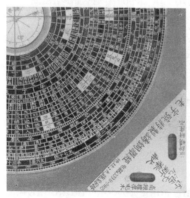

There can be up to 36 rings including the Eight Trigrams, the Ten Heavenly Stems, the Twelve Earthly Branches (Chinese Zodiac), the Five Elements, the Nine Moving Stars, the Seventy-Two Dragons, the Nine Palaces of the Hidden Stem (for determining the Magic Square), the Sixty-Four Hexagrams of the *I Ching* and more. Using the compass you can get a very precise reading of the Qi energy. This information is compared with a person's astrological chart to see if there is harmony or disharmony between the home and the person.

popular both in China and the United States. It is one of the oldest systems of Feng Shui and is still practiced in China today. It takes into consideration the topography of the land, flow of roads, placement of neighboring buildings, architecture of the house and the needs of the people living inside. In Form School, harmony and livability are of utmost importance. Anything that is not aesthetically pleasing is considered "not beneficial" (in other words, it will not improve the flow of Qi).

I have taken the classic and sometimes rigid rules of Feng Shui and translated them into doable concepts for today's Western lifestyles, homes, community structures and everyday environments. The principles in this book can readily be applied to your personal environment. With this guidebook to refer to, you will be able to make your house truly your home.

Before we launch into the rest of this book, here is a brief explanation of the other schools of Feng Shui, traditions that have developed in the East over the past 2,000 years. You will find a number of Chinese words and cultural concepts in the text below. The main focus of this section is to provide a glimpse into how the various schools of thought differ from one another.

Compass School Feng Shui

Compass School and Form School are the two schools of Feng Shui practiced today in China. Compass School practitioners use a special compass (called a lo–pan; see fig. 1) for measuring Qi. This special compass consists of six to thirty–six rings, usually inscribed with Chinese characters, with a working compass in the center (called The Well of Heaven). Two red threads, attached to the square base (called earth), cross the compass at perpendicular angles. The Feng Shui expert lines up the threads with the walls of the house, then moves the round center plate (called heaven) until the needle of the compass lines up with south.

Note: South is considered the principle direction in China and in Feng Shui. On Chinese maps, south is "up" whereas our Western–made maps place north at the top. Since many of the more important centers of civilization in China (cities, ports and population) were to the south, it is not surprising from a cultural perspective that south would be given its position of importance on maps—at the top.

The Five Elements

Wood symbolizes growth and creativity. It is represented by tall thin shapes like a tree trunk, things made of wood and the color green.

Fire symbolizes intelligence and energy. It is represented by triangular shapes, things made of plastic and the color red.

Earth symbolizes endurance and stability. It is represented by table–like shapes, things made of clay and stone, and the color yellow.

Metal symbolizes wealth and business acumen. It is represented by the round coin shape, things made of metal and the color white.

Water symbolizes movement and communication. It is represented by irregular and undulating shapes, things made of glass and the color blue.

Once the compass is aligned, the information along the red threads is read and interpreted. Rings of I Ching, trigrams and hexagrams, types of dragons, stems and branches, water features and constellations make up the information that is delineated during the interpretation. The precise combination of all of these considerations provides the basis for determining the quality and quantity of Qi present in a particular environment. This Qi can then be enhanced with "cures." (See Cures, pp. 137.)

Elemental School Feng Shui

This system can be combined with other systems to enhance the art of precise placement of objects and the selection of colors or materials. The goal of the Elemental system is to balance the five elements: wood, earth, metal, fire, and water. These are the same elements that form the basis for Chinese medicine, the Chinese Zodiac and other cultural practices.

Each element has a shape, a color and a natural material associated with it. These elements can exist in a creative cycle or in a destructive cycle with one another—in other words, they can act upon each other to either help or hinder the movement of Qi, thus affecting the ambiance of a home.

A Feng Shui practitioner of the Elemental School determines how the elements of the site, the home, the décor and the people living within the house interact with each other. Symbols of the elements can then either be added to or removed from the environment to create balance and harmony.

Flying Star School Feng Shui

The Flying Star system of Feng Shui has gained recent popularity. Each "star" represents a different quality of energy for a period of time based on the Chinese Lunar Calendar. The changes are structured to conform to a two–year, twenty–year and sixty–year cycle. Practitioners then base the Feng Shui analysis of the rooms and the placement of any furniture or décor on a person's personal star and the timeliness of that star.

Black Hat Compass

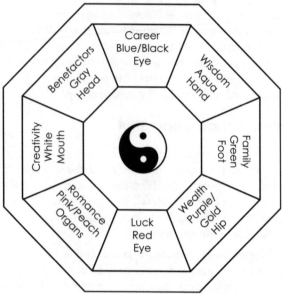

Fig. 2: Ba–gua compass is not a compass that indicates directions like north and south, rather it locates the "life stations," the areas of life energy in the house. A life station area can be enhanced with special cures to bring more energy to that aspect of life. The octagon is laid over the floor plan with Career at the main door to the house. The ba–gua remains fixed in this same position for all floors of the building. The ba–gua can be stretched if the building is not a perfect square. With this map you can determine which room corresponds to which life station.

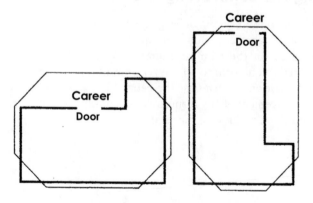

Black Hat School Feng Shui

The Black Hat system of Feng Shui is a fairly recent invention and has become wildly popular in the past few years here in the West. It can be categorized as a simplified form of the Compass School, but it borrows from the Form and Elemental Schools as well.

The Black Hat system is generally used on existing structures. Floor plans are divided into eight different segments using an octagon called a ba–gua compass (see fig. 2). Literally translated, ba–gua means "eight symbols of divination." The ba–gua compass is oriented so that one of those symbols—the one that represents a person's career—is placed at the front door or main entrance to the home, building or other structure. Then the other symbols on the ba–gua are laid out in a consistent pattern.

The Feng Shui practitioner, using this technique, determines the quantity and quality of the energy in a given location of the house (wealth, fame, relationship, children, benefactors, knowledge, wisdom and health). Then cures are placed in the appropriate areas of the house to stimulate *Qi*.

Again, all systems are valid and most have been used successfully for hundreds or even thousands of years. In this book we are going to adhere to the Form School, the one I believe best combines aesthetic style with logical sense.

What is a Cure?

One term you will encounter everywhere as you discover the many aspects of Feng Shui, is cure. There are nine categories of cures and each one has a different use or application in Feng Shui. (These are fully discussed in Chapters 8-16.) Some cures are effective in a variety of different situations, while others can be used only for very specific purposes. The manner in which we select or "place" cures is similar to the way an acupuncturist places the healing needles that stimulate personal *Qi*. Throughout this book we will discuss a variety of specific cures in the context of using Feng Shui to increase benefits in our lives.

When starting out, the most important thing to know about cures is that when a cure is placed or used correctly, changes happen quickly. If a cure is not placed or used correctly, then nothing happens—or, in rare cases, things can get worse. However, even with this warning in mind, never be afraid to experiment. Just be aware of your surroundings and your intuition as you work to balance Q*i* in your environment. Should things take a turn for the worse, simply move the cure, or test an alternative cure to balance and improve the energy.

As you choose and place cures, Feng Shui Form School tradition dictates that the placement must be aesthetically pleasing for the cure to be effective. In other words, if the cure doesn't look good, if it looks out of place, if you are bumping into it, or banging your head on it—well, then your cure is probably in the wrong place.

In each chapter of this book we will discuss the guidelines of good Feng Shui, things that have worked for successful practitioners and millions of satisfied people over a long period of time. We will explore a variety of common yet disruptive factors we often encounter in our Western environments and examine a wide variety of possible cures to apply in these instances—cures to facilitate the flow of Q*i*. Our objective is to create harmony and balance in our unique environments and in our lives.

Chapter 2

Welcome to the Neighborhood!

The first step to any good Feng Shui process is to persuade the Qi that exists in the earth and in the space between heaven and earth to enter our front doors and enrich our lives. Take a moment to consider all of the geographical and ecological diversity that exists on our earth. Some places are lush and fertile, some are forests with waterfalls, some consist of dry desert valleys and some have tall mountains so high that no vegetation grows on the peaks. Some places are devoid of human habitation; others, packed with humanity—life in all its forms seemingly in constant motion. All of these places are representations of the different aspects of Qi. When Qi is strong (Yang), one can feel the vibrancy of life all around; where Qi is weak (Yin), there is quiet, a lack of vibrant physicality. When Qi moves very quickly, people (and things) move quickly. When Qi moves slowly, the rhythm of life is more relaxed; life moves at a calm and regulated pace.

You have certainly felt the differences in Qi in the places you visit on a regular basis. Let us think about a couple of places we all are familiar with. For instance, think of the different kinds of places where people can put their money. First, there is the bank. Banks have very slow Qi, the atmosphere is calm and sedate. They are often decorated in a style that seems to say, "We are important, safe, respectable and serious about our responsibility to you, and to your money." Every time we walk into a bank, we feel this Qi and therefore we feel that our money (the money in our savings and checking accounts or the valuables in our safe–deposit boxes) is protected, safe from any harm. Casinos are another example of places where people take their money. Casinos are loud, glittery and filled with all manner of spinning apparatus making every imaginable sound as the money Qi moves around. The Qi in a casino moves very quickly; it guides us right up to the machines and tables, keeping us hypnotized with the spinning lights and colors. The energy here is fun and exciting. There is the promise (or at least the hope) that if we just plunk down a few dollars we may walk out with our pockets stuffed with cash. In these venues, the bank and the casino, the Qi is clearly identifiable. In both, the nature and flow of Qi is created entirely by the décor.

It is also true that some banks do better than others and likewise some casinos. This is based on the flow or quality of the Qi in the physical environment, and quantity of Qi inside the bank or casino. The same thing happens with our homes—sometimes the Qi in our location is in harmony and supports the kinds of opportunities, people and things we want to attract, but sometimes the energy is counterproductive, even destructive, and we feel blocked from the very things we wish to manifest or experience in our lives.

When we can identify an area where businesses or homes are well-maintained and the environment seems prosperous, we know we have found an area of sheng Qi (good Qi). Who can argue with success? Though a buyer may find the best prices in the dilapidated neighborhoods, there may be sha Qi (negative Qi) in the area and it could be the reason for the appearance of the property. Good Qi energizes people and it attracts money and opportunities for these people to enjoy. One of the easiest ways to identify good Qi is to find a "good" neighborhood.

If you are not one of the fortunate individuals living in a neighborhood with good Qi, then you will have to make additional effort to shift or change the existing energy location if you want to receive all of the benefits inherent in an environment filled with good Qi. Unbelievable as it may sound, a single individual can shift or change the energy of her own home (and her own life); sometimes all it takes is one individual to shift the flow of the Qi in the whole neighborhood. I am going to show you how to be that person.

My Neighborhood

Defining "neighborhood" is an interesting exercise in semantics. How would you define the concept neighborhood? Think about it for a moment. To some people it means a few houses near their own, the people who live in the houses directly next door to or across the street from their own dwelling. Some people, on the other hand, define their neighborhoods as consisting of a few (or several) surrounding blocks from their own residences in one or more directions.

From a Feng Shui perspective the neighborhood comprises the area you can see from the front, back and sides of your property. The concept is that if you can see it from your property, it can affect your property. Since surrounding buildings, structures, roads, waterways, mountains, hills and people can affect the Qi in one's home and family, we need to consider everything that is around a residence as "the neighborhood."

Now apply this concept to your neighborhood again. Are the houses well–maintained (a sign of good Qi) or are the yards overgrown and the homes unkempt? Do you know if the houses in your neighborhood have increased in value over the past few years, or has there been a decline in sales amounts? If there has been a decline, you definitely want to change the Qi energy of your home and neighborhood. You can change the flow of Qi in your neighborhood as you change the energy in your own yard and home. Is industry or commercial enterprise encroaching on your residential neighborhood (or visa versa)? Industrial or commercial businesses can cause a shift in traffic patterns and may even change the types of people who come through your neighborhood on their way to or from an activity nearby. On the other hand, a trend of creating high–end condominiums in industrial areas has breathed new life into some dead Qi zones.

Here are a few basic Feng Shui rules for neighborhoods. If you identify problems in your neighborhood, don't panic, simply focus on the cures suggested below.

Rule #1: Large buildings take Qi away from smaller buildings. If your house is situated next to a building (including another house) that is substantially larger than yours, your neighbor—no matter what his intentions are—is sucking the Qi away from your house. This will cause you to need to work harder for everything: making a living, keeping your job, and maintaining your relationships with the people who are important in your life. It will cause your spouse (or significant other) and children (and anyone else who lives in your house) to work harder as well.

Your house is affected when the house or building next door is at least twice the size of your own (size may be determined either by height or square footage). So, if your neighbor's house is two stories tall and yours is a single story, then your house is losing *Qi* to your neighbor. Likewise if you have a nice 1,500 square foot house but the house next door to yours is 3,000 square feet or more, that neighboring house is receiving energy that should be yours.

Houses or buildings that can affect yours are usually the ones on either side. But Feng Shui also takes into consideration the house across the street or the one directly behind you. If the bigger building is extremely large or tall—for example, an apartment, condominium or business complex—then it may be located a few doors down from your residence and yet still affect your *Qi*. Your home is significantly affected if the distance to the building is less than its height. In other words, if the building were to fall onto its side and hit your property line, then you are losing substantial *Qi*.

Your residence is also affected if there is a clear line of sight between you and the very large house or building. Even when there is a tree or two, a wall, a fence, a really robust bush between your home and the other one, it doesn't matter. If you can clearly see the larger house/building from your property, then it is affecting you and yours.

To remedy this situation, we need to "reflect back" the grasping, grabbing energy to the source from which it comes. When you take this action, you will be able to keep the energy (and the benefits) you work so hard to attract into your life. Suddenly life will be easier for you and the people under your roof. You will be able to breathe, to relax and enjoy the fruits of your labor.

Cure: A mirror is the solution. Take a small mirror, one less than eight inches across. You can choose mirrors specifically designed for this Feng Shui purpose or you can select a simple round or square mirror. This mirror needs to be placed on the outside of your house facing the offending building (or it can be placed in a window facing out towards the problem structure). Remember, line of sight is an important consideration. The mirror should be placed high enough to provide a clear view over any fences or walls around your property. Once you have placed a mirror to reflect back the draining *Qi* of the larger building, leave it there permanently. The chapter on mirrors will outline these concepts in more detail.

Rule #2: Churches, as with all large buildings, take Qi away from smaller buildings. The main reason for this rule is the same as the one we learned about in Rule #1; churches are usually very large/tall buildings, and so naturally, *Qi* is attracted to them. Second, it is said that people go to church to release their sins. From a traditional Feng Shui perspective, sins released inside the walls of a church will go next door (or to any door they can easily "find") and visit your house.

Cure: The solution is the same as the one described above. Place a mirror facing the church to reflect back the *Qi* created by the church, the steeple and the size of the building. The mirror should be placed in a similar manner as described above. This will not harm the church in any way, it will simply protect the *Qi* you are trying to attract into your own home.

Rule #3: Sharp angles of other buildings should not point towards the flat sides of your house. These sharp angles are called poison arrows (see fig. 3). A poison arrow is a protruding corner or edge of a neighboring building that directs very sharp, pointed *Qi* at your house. From the perspective of Feng Shui, we will always feel safer if something sharp is not pointed at us.

Having a poison arrow attacking your house constantly stirs up difficult *Qi* for those living in the house. It can cause everyone in the dwelling to be at cross purposes or to commit acts of self–sabotage (anything from addictions to maintaining bad habits in general). It can cause people living in the house to argue excessively, to sever ties and to create resentments.

Example: I once consulted on a ranch–style house in California where the couple was on the verge of a divorce due to constant fighting. To make matters worse, the previous owners of the house had divorced while living there, so the house had a history that included couples actively involved in confrontational behavior towards one another. One walk around my client's property revealed that a neighboring house, a tall, modern–style home, had been built at an angle on the adjoining property. One of the sharp angles of this neighboring home was attacking my client's residence.

External Poison Arrows

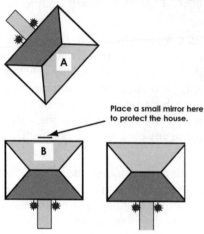

Place a small mirror here to protect the house.

Fig. 3: External poison arrows are present when houses or buildings are set at angles to one another. Here house A is attacking house B. The solution is to place a mirror on house B to protect it from the attacking house.

Fig. 4: Houses on a cul-de-sac can attack other houses as the corners point at each other. Plant foliage between houses to protect from the negative energy of poison arrows.

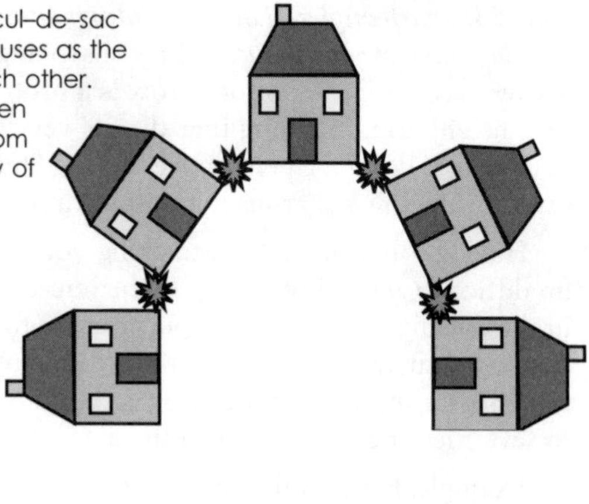

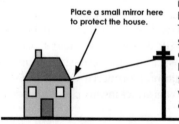

Place a small mirror here to protect the house.

Fig. 5: Electrical lines that come into the house at a right angle bring negative energy with it. To protect the house place a small mirror on the house in the direction of the electrical lines. Have the mirror pointing towards the electrical pole. This will help deflect the negative energy.

I placed the appropriate cures and two weeks later I received a note from the wife thanking me and letting me know that she and her husband had started counseling and that they both felt the future looked very promising for them to work out their disagreements and stay together.

Cure: If a corner of a neighbor's house points at the flat side of your home and there are no trees, no walls, nothing between that corner and your house, you are receiving the *Qi* of a poison arrow. The best cure is to place something living between your home and the offending corner, such as a tree or large bush. If this is not possible, then place a mirror on your home pointing directly at the protruding corner. This will neutralize the difficult energy of the poison arrow. The placing of this mirror should follow the rules listed above. (See also Chapter 9, Mirrors.)

Rule #4: Do not place mirrors on all four sides of your house or building. While mirrors represent protection, too much protection turns your home into a fortress, not allowing any *Qi* to enter. In extreme cases the result may be that all income stops, opportunities cannot reach the people who live in the house and relationships become stagnant and lifeless. Always leave at least one side "open" to allow *Qi* to find a way into your home. And, if you have a business at home, avoid all but the most necessary mirror placements to allow the maximum amount of business *Qi* to find you (whether business comes to you through your front door, via the telephone, fax or Internet).

The following rules and suggestions are for special circumstances.

Living on a dead–end street or cul–de–sac. Personally, I love cul–de–sac living. I love the neighborly feeling and the security of living in a tight neighborhood. However, here are a few things to watch for when living on a closed–end street:

The big sign at the entrance to a cul–de–sac often states in bold letters, "Dead End Street." This is not an auspicious sign to see when driving into your neighborhood. It is unfortunate that some cities choose this wording instead of "No Outlet," "No Through Way" or, better still, "Private." If you have a progressive city planner where you live it might be possible to propose that the city change the "Dead End" wording to something a little more favorable.

If the sign cannot be changed, make sure you place living things in your yard to represent life force *Qi*, making it clear that you will not accept anything "dead" in your house. Having living plants or healthy trees is a good idea. Also, make a little extra effort to feed the birds and welcome the neighborhood pets. You may even want to place small statues depicting animals or children in your front yard.

Poison arrows can be quite common in cul–de–sacs (see fig. 4). Since the layout of a cul–de–sac is usually a street ending in a semi–circle of houses, there are often some houses at the end of the cul–de–sac beaming poison arrows at each other. Now, if the corner of one house points at a corner of another house, then they are in effect neutralizing the negative energy each one sends out to the other. But if the corner of one of the other houses points at a flat side of your house, then you have a problem and you should consider one of the cures listed above for poison arrows.

Example: I actually lived in a neighborhood at the end of a cul–de–sac. The houses on either side of my own home had corners pointing at each other. Interestingly, the owners of the houses were mother and daughter–in–law, and even though the relationship between the two women was friendly, it was very, very active. All day long people would walk back and forth from one house to the other; there was constant interaction between the members of the two households, lots of visiting and gossip. If the corner of your house points to the corner of a neighbor and there are no plants, trees or walls to break up the flow of *Qi* between the two houses, expect a lot of interaction between yourself and that particular neighbor.

Generally speaking, the house at the end of the cul–de–sac can be in the path of too much *Qi*. Think of the road leading to the houses as if it were a pathway for all *Qi* flowing into the cul–de–sac. If a car on the road were to lose its brakes, would it crash into the house at the end of the cul–de–sac? The *Qi* flowing into the neighborhood moves with the same type of force you would experience from a car with no breaks as it reaches the end of a road. Houses at the end of a cul–de–sac are often bombarded with too much energy. The result is often that people in the house experience a lot of stress; they have little or no personal free time;

they are constantly busy with work, careers, kids and hobbies. They can drive themselves to exhaustion.

Cure: As I said above, I lived in a house at the end of a cul–de–sac. The energy did not hit my house because there was a walled courtyard in front. My front yard had a large tree (not directly in front of the door), lots of bushes and plants and a fountain. This type of cure shields the house from excess Qi.

Some houses in a cul–de–sac receive more positive Qi than others. The energy moves the way traffic moves, so in the United States the houses on the right (as you enter the cul–de–sac) receive an abundance of fresh, new Qi. The Qi then enters the circle at the end of the street and slows (this is the area where cars can turn around). Then any remaining Qi makes its way out along the left side of the cul–de–sac. The first houses on the right receive a normal amount of energy. The houses at the beginning of the circle receive the best possible amount of energy, and the houses on the left receive whatever is left over. The lesser amount of Qi received by the house, the lower the energy levels of the people living within the house will be, and the harder they will have to work to get what they want from life.

Cure: We all want the best quantity and quality of Qi no matter the location of our homes. We can add a set of wind chimes to the front of the house to attract and move the Qi inside. (You can read more about the different types of wind chimes and the best ones for attracting this type of energy in the Cures section of this book, pp. 166.) Choose the best type of wind chime to attract the Qi you and other family members need. For the purpose of calling Qi, wind chimes should be placed either on the front porch or in the front yard—hang them from a tree, light, fence or even the mailbox. You are making an effort to catch the Qi as it passes by so place the wind chime where it can be both seen from both the street and the front door of your home.

Living at the top of a "T" intersection. Because traffic/Qi/energy travels in a straight line, unless there's an obstacle in the way, when it approaches the top of the "T" it blasts the house sitting there. These houses tend to become rental homes because the Qi is too intense for most people to tolerate. It becomes difficult for people to live in such a home for any extended period of time. A cure is definitely necessary in these cases.

Cure: There should be a tree, a wall or a fence between the street and the front door. This will help protect the house from negative Qi. However, if there is a tree, it shouldn't be in direct line with the door or else it will be just as disruptive a force as the traffic pattern in the street. While the tree does protect from the aggressive on–coming Qi, it ends up protecting so well that all Qi is blocked from reaching the front door. If you are not fortunate enough to have a tree in your front yard, a wall or fence between you and oncoming traffic you can further mellow the Qi hitting your T–intersection house by hanging bells or wind chimes from the porch. The bells or the rods of the chime should be made of shiny brass. This will act like a mirrored tube bouncing the Qi into the environment all around. Some of this excess Qi will go back to the road and some will come into the house. This will create a balance of Qi, calming things down for the people living in the house.

Living in a home on the corner. If your house is on a corner, it is more exposed yet Qi seems to pass it by. The Qi flows with the traffic and needs extra incentive to stop at your house. Without that Qi it is more vulnerable and statistics say that a house on a corner is broken into or vandalized more often than other residences in a block of houses. So, a house on the corner needs both to collect good Qi and defend against negative Qi more than other houses.

Cure: To collect the good Qi hang a concave mirror in front of the house facing the street. This concave shape allows Qi to collect and pool. Then to defend against negative Qi the best protection cure would be a logical, practical one such as a fence or wall along the exposed side of the house. If that is not possible, then a classic protection mirror such as a traditional ba–gua is the best defense. (You will find a picture of this mirror on pp. 151.) Place your protection mirror in a window on an exposed side of the house and set it facing the street.

Chapter 3

Home and Garden

Qi must find your house in order to energize it. If people cannot find your house, chances are that *Qi* cannot either. Here are some tips for houses that are difficult to find:

Situation: The hard to find house. If your house is hard to find because it is in a remote location, back in the woods, up a long dirt road (or if we would need a native guide to lead us to it), you will need to give the *Qi* some help getting to your house. You can do this by identifying or placing visible landmarks to help the *Qi* find a path to your door. Landmarks can be signs, statues, ribbons—anything that stands out and clearly denotes that there is a house at the end of the road. The same things that attract people will attract *Qi*. Create a clear outline with directions leading to your home that will easily convey to another how to get there. If it happens that you always have to go out to meet someone halfway and guide them to your house, you will also find you need to meet every opportunity halfway because the *Qi* just can't make it to your door; this can be quite exhausting after a while.

Cure: We all need *Qi* to find our homes but if you live in a remote location you will need to set up a path for the *Qi* to follow on its way to the house. This can be accomplished using clear quartz crystals. (You may try using other rocks or gems, but the quality and quantity of *Qi* that comes your way will vary greatly. See the section Crystals, pp. 141, for more information.) Clear quartz crystals channel *Qi*. We have been using crystals in radios, watches and other devices for a hundred years or more, in fact a simple crystal radio needs no batteries or other power sources to work. Now you can use this energy to direct *Qi* towards your home. Plant small tumbled clear quartz crystals (they will look somewhat round, like a river rock) on either side of the road to your house. Plant them in pairs like lights on an airport runway; plant them in the ground so only the tops are showing. The number of crystals needed varies depending on the distance from your house to the point where it gets confusing (where you meet the native guide). Plant them as close together as you like but no further than

500 feet apart. It is also a good idea to check on them every few months (and after the spring thaw in cold climates) to make sure that the tops are still exposed.

Example: I am a transplant to the city of Boston by way of Los Angeles, California and Albuquerque, New Mexico. So I am used to finding my way around a city built on a grid. It was a complete shock to me when I first began to attempt to navigate the streets of Boston and Massachusetts. For instance, if one misses or passes by one's destination in Boston, there is no simple 'drive around the block and try again' remedy because there are no blocks, just endless winding streets—scenic, yes; easy, no. In these situations we may need to help people and *Qi* find their destination. The best way to do this is to map out a precise set of instructions to give potential visitors, using accurate distances and landmarks as guidelines (if there are more than 4,000 donut shops in a square mile radius then the donut shop may not be a good landmark). To help the *Qi* find your home, identify or place something at the front of the house that makes a statement as if to say: "This is the house; you've found it." This could be a statue, a special tree, a flag or an architectural feature. Having a positive identification marker will attract an abundance of good *Qi* to the residence.

Situation: A home surrounded by identical houses. If your house is hard to find because it is surrounded by identical houses, then you need to make your home stand out in some way without breaking association rules or annoying the neighbors. This can be tricky in closed communities.

Cure: Colored flags, special door mats, wreathes of plant material on the door, chimes, bird feeders, or your name on a plaque near the entrance, any or all of these cures will help direct *Qi* to your door rather than having it be diffused and scattered among so many neighbors.

The Yard

Now let us move in closer to your residence. I love seeing people's houses inside and out, and I wish I could see yours. But in the meantime, I want you to see your house with new eyes—the eyes of a Feng Shui expert.

Path to the Door

Fig. 6: The curved path to the front door is considered more auspicious as it gives the *Qi* a pleasant way to your door. A very straight path will cause the *Qi* to move very quickly, forcing the family to feel rushed and often unprepared for opportunities.

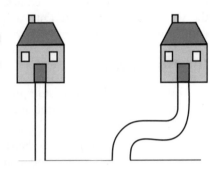

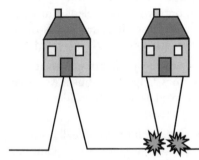

Fig. 7: Both walkways shown here choke the *Qi*. The one that narrows at the door cuts off the flow of opportunities before they can reach the family. While the second, with its narrow entrance blocked by foliage, stops energy from even entering the property.

Fig. 8: If the entrance is blocked by a tree or a telephone pole then the *Qi* will not be able to find the door. The family will also feel blocked and have trouble taking direct action to achieve what they want. It is bad luck, however, to cut down a live tree. The best solution is to relocate the tree to the back yard.

If you have no control over the yard surrounding your home, and cannot choose what is planted there, cannot add or subtract anything, cannot add as much as a single garden gnome (not that there is a lot of Feng Shui lore connected with gnomes), then skip this section and move on to Entryways, pp. 53. But for the rest of you, let us start in the front yard.

The Front Yard

Your front yard is the first impression of you and your family that the world sees. Its condition and appearance will either attract or repel good *Qi*.

Rule #1: Maintain the general appearance of your yard. Weather permitting and this book in hand, take a walk in your yard. Really look at the outside of your home. Feel the kind of impression your house makes from every angle. In Form School Feng Shui aesthetics are very important. If something looks pleasant, it attracts positive *Qi*; if something looks cluttered, untidy or disheveled, it attracts poor or negative *Qi*. Worst case scenario, if your yard is often mistaken for a demolition site then disruptive *Qi* is attracted.

Cure: Things do not have to be pristine, perfect or new to attract good energy, but tidy certainly does help. Trim bushes so that walkways are clear, keep grass (or weeds) cut, and consider ground cover, like rocks or mulch, in bare areas.

Rule #2: Attractive environments attract more Qi. Ideally, a front yard should have a winding path to the front door, plantings appropriate to the climate and location and some sort of decoration that makes the house unique in the neighborhood. Let us begin with the path to the front door—it should be clear. People and *Qi* will be coming to your front door and it is not good if they must vault over lawn furniture, step around toys and cut their way through thorny bushes or plants. Keep the bushes well–trimmed (especially if they have sharp, pointy ends); keep toys and clutter to an absolute minimum; and keep the path clear of debris (anything that might cause visitors to stumble or lose their footing on their way from the street to the front door).

Having a winding path leading to the front door is preferable to having a straight one (see fig. 6). A straight path moves the *Qi* very quickly—and as most of us will attest, our lives are moving too fast as it is. Slow the movement of the *Qi* down with a winding path which then, much like a meandering river, serves to balance the flow of energy to the house and its inhabitants. However, it is not a good idea to have a path that winds so much that people cut across the lawn to save time getting to the front door. The perfect pathway curves just enough that it only takes a few extra steps to arrive at the destination.

The entrance to the path should not be smaller than the width of the front door (see fig. 7). The size of your front door (both of them, if you have a double door) defines the amount of *Qi* that can comfortably enter your home. The homes of the wealthy usually have a double door at the front of their residences, and the people living in these homes are often offered greater opportunities in life. If you have a double door to your home, you need to have a double wide path as well. If your path starts out narrow, from the street or driveway to your home, *Qi* is choked off right at the start and much less can actually get to your front door, hence into your life.

When we consider all of the different climates and environments in the various places around our earth, we realize that there are an endless combination of trees, bushes, plants and grasses to choose from as we create the beauty in our yards. The lore and meanings of individual plants, blossoms and trees would fill many volumes. (See Living Cures, pp. 181 for more on the symbolism of a few trees and plants.) I will discuss only a few general rules about plants in this section of the book.

Cures: If you have living plants anywhere in your environment, they need to be healthy to attract positive *Qi*. If you live in a part of the United States that is not conducive to easily growing things (like a desert or in downtown metropolis) it is perfectly fine to have a front yard without plantings. However, if you decide that you are going to have plants, they need to be living ones.

The first and most important step in enhancing your yard to attract positive *Qi* is to remove dead trees, bushes, plants, etc., immediately. If you are uncertain whether or not one of your plants is alive, find someone to ask. If the plants or trees look dead but are living, keep them and spend some time caring for them. However, if a tree is threatening the safety of the house (i.e., it could come crashing down into your house during a storm or earthquake, or the root system is spreading into your plumbing and/or affecting the foundation of the house) have it removed. Otherwise, it is considered bad luck to cut down a living tree. If the tree is small enough and you don't want it in your yard, consider having it transplanted. (There may be a gardening service in your area that provides tree removal free of charge or at a minimal fee if they are allowed to sell the tree to another of their clients.)

Now that I have made every effort to convince you to keep your trees, I must say that having a tree directly in line with your front door is not considered lucky (see fig. 8). If the trunk of the tree lines up exactly with the front door, there will be problems with the circulation of Qi. In this instance it is best to place an energy deflector between your door and the tree. Such a deflector might be a wind chime with shiny, round rod–shaped chimes. The rods act as round mirrors disbursing negative Qi, and they also chime harmoniously, calling in positive Qi.

A healthy tree in the front yard symbolizes your children's future success (and for those of you who do not have children, it symbolizes the success of your creative projects, your art, your novel and your pets). Trees to the left or right of the house protect and guard the house. Trees at the back of the house bring support from others and benefit all of your endeavors.

Rule #3: "Lawn Art" Matters. What does it mean to have a yard littered with hot pink flamingos? Believe it or not, the ancient Chinese texts on Feng Shui do not have a lot of details about hot pink flamingos however, they do mention the power of the images of birds. Birds represent successful relationships—especially when birds are found in pairs. The Chinese texts also explore the significance of color in our lives and relate colors to the movement of Qi. We, here in the West, have many both traditional and modern views about colors. Every good landscape designer takes color choices into consideration before making any other decisions about a project. In this case, pink is a passive color, giving the impression of gentle submissiveness. Choosing the brighter shade of the color definitely will attract attention. Therefore the bright pink flamingos announce to the world that you are looking for love and you are really completely harmless. This may or may not be the message you wanted to send.

Using the principles of Feng Shui, it is possible to look at a yard and read the messages inherent in the symbols that are placed there—intentionally or accidentally—and identify the type of *Qi* that is being attracted to the home and its inhabitants. In many instances people may not be aware of the type of *Qi* they are attracting, and it is also possible that the *Qi* that is being attracted is not the type they want to bring into their lives. It takes a lot of force to counter any *Qi* that the yard is making such an effort to pull in. So, when you study your yard and the lawn art you have chosen, it is worth a little extra effort to examine exactly what message is going out into the world around you. In short, your yard art should symbolize the energy you want to attract.

There are many different kinds of energy that people can attract using lawn art, so let us start with ones everyone can identify with. For instance, we may wish to attract comfort, wealth, happy relationships, good health or joy. Begin with these and later you can expand and attract more.

Cures: The best symbol for attracting comfort is a welcoming chair or bench placed attractively in the front yard. Ideally place it where it's a bit shady and where someone sitting in it would be offered a nice view of flowers or trees. The energy represented by a comfortable seat attracts comforting *Qi* to the home and family.

The best lawn art for attracting wealth is a functioning fountain. A fountain placed in the front yard will attract new opportunities for career activities and wealth in general. The moving water creates a flow of *Qi* bringing one beneficial opportunity after another. A fountain should be placed so it is closer to your front door than to a neighbor's front door. It should be in proportion to the size of the house. (So, a modest house should have a modest fountain.)

Example: I consulted with a family who said they had constructed a large, handmade concrete fountain in their front yard. I hurried over to see it and found a fountain so large it obscured the house. The couple who lived there owned a business that had expanded much too quickly and had totally spun out of their control; there were filing cabinets in their bedroom, and the hallways, orders piled by the door went unfilled and the phone rang non–stop. Finally, stressed to the point of needing treatment for ulcers and other health concerns, they started making costly mistakes in their business. The excessively large fountain was bombarding the house with Qi and the solution was to get a jackhammer and reduce the size of the fountain.

In general, fountains need to be flowing for at least a short time every week to be an effective cure. It is all right to move or cover fountains in winter (freeing temperatures can pulverize a concrete fountain). Other prosperity cures and symbols can be placed in the house specifically in winter to compensate for the loss of the fountain's effectiveness during the coldest months of the year. (Fountains can also be placed inside the house, but that will be discussed in Chapter 12, Moving Cures.)

The symbols on a fountain or the message symbolized by the fountain itself are important as they attract Qi, so look for abundant happy symbols for your prosperity fountain. For instance, fountains that depict little boys peeing into ponds (a very common fountain motif) may represent the way you handle the money that comes into your life. As mentioned previously, birds symbolize relationships, as do maidens, love goddesses and flowers. Basic, unadorned fountains attract money and prosperity, as do fountains with fish designs (also scales, dolphins, starfish and shells). Try to find out the meaning behind the design of any fountain you choose. If there are Chinese characters on the fountain, take the time to find out what these mean to make sure the concepts they represent are in harmony with the Qi you are trying to attract into your life.

Example: Dry river beds represent the possibility of the flow of wealth and can be used in desert landscaping. At one tract house that had been xeriscaped, a dry river bed had been artistically created in different color rocks. This depiction of a "river" split into two smaller "streams" near the path to the front door. Ultimately, the image that had been created looked like a huge snake with its mouth open, swallowing up whomever approached the house. After rearranging the colored rocks, we turned the "snake" into a flower and the family's luck changed immediately.

The best lawn art for attracting love is the birdfeeder. Other love and relationship symbols include statues of ducks (pairs of mandarin ducks are believed to strengthen a relationship and make it last), bunnies (believed to bring new babies into the home) and deer (thought to enhance intuition and can help those who live in the house discern whether new people they meet are friend or foe). (See Chapter 11, Living Cures.)

Plants and flowers are proven cures to attract good health and well–being. Planting herbs is even better; traditionally they are known to support health and have been used for such purposes in every culture—in fact, just having some growing in the garden helps the energy of health.

The Chinese place pagodas in their gardens to bring peace and to make the home a sacred space. If you are looking to enhance this type of Qi in your life, you could place a large or small pagoda in your yard (it should be in proportion with the yard and the house). A pagoda can be made from stone or clay (I have also seen ones made from metal and glass and those are fine too); they can be placed in either the front or back yard. If you have a pagoda, harmonize the other lawn art with it. Even the most attractive pagoda loses its effectiveness in a yard filled with garden gnomes and pink flamingos.

"Gazing balls" were popular many years ago and are now once again showing up in landscape design. A gazing ball is a highly–reflective, colored ball ranging from the size of a softball to a basketball. It sits on a pedestal in the garden, acting like a mirror cure—reflecting away negativity from every angle. The gazing ball is a colorful addition to any garden; though it is usually placed in the back yard, it can be quite at home in the front yard as well. This decorative item is believed to protect against bad spirits and negative Qi.

Back and Side Yards

Sometimes it is a good idea to take a look at familiar places with fresh eyes. Take a look at your back yard. Stand in your yard with your back to the house. What do you see? Is there a wall or fence between your yard and that of your neighbor? Are there residences or does your land back into some industrial or commercial property? Does your property back into a rising hill? Or, is there a forest, a pond, a road, an alley? Each of these represent a particular Qi energy.

Rule #1: The ideal is to have a rising hill behind your property. This would, according to the precepts of Feng Shui, protect your property from the elements (and the barbarian hordes that once tended to sneak up on the citizens of peaceful Chinese villages in ancient times). If a small hill is behind your property, your home receives lots of supportive *Qi* and is defended from negative energy of all kinds. Since the home is "safe," this allows the members of the household to go out into the world filled with confidence, knowing they will receive the support they need in the ventures they pursue.

Instead of a rising hill, you may have a fence or wall surrounding your yard. The fence provides protection from strangers, holds back some of the negative energy that may be around you, creates a boundary between neighbors, and prevents you from accidentally mowing their lawn.

Cure: If nothing separates your property from that of your neighbors, then metaphorically your back is unprotected. Consider creating a boundary between you and your neighbors. If you are having trouble with neighbors, it is certainly wise to consider a fence or wall.

If your house backs up to industrial or commercial land, then you could certainly have a problem with maintaining balanced *Qi* in your life. Industrial buildings are usually larger than residential ones, and the larger building will "drink up" all of the *Qi* in the entire area. Businesses can change quickly from quiet, unassuming neighbors, to being the hub of a multinational enterprise—bringing trucks, noise and other environmental disturbances, and further draining the *Qi* from your property. This usually lowers property values in the neighborhood and disturbs the harmony of your site. If your home does back up to a building that is much larger than your own, build at the very least a tall fence or wall. This will help to diminish the amount of *Qi* that is drained from your property. Or, even better, build a wall, then place a line of trees along the inside of your wall and add a protection mirror to the outside of your house pointing at the offending building.

Rule #2: Balance out "Heaven and Earth." The basic principle of Feng Shui is to bring wind (representing the concept heaven) and water (representing the concept earth) into harmony and balance. Both heaven and earth are represented by shapes—heaven is a round shape and earth is square. We can balance out these two energies by adding these shapes to your back yard.

Cure: Your back yard, in general, should be laid out to suit your needs: vegetables, herbs and flowers for the gardening enthusiast, play equipment for the kids and/or a pool, hot tub, barbeque, game area for the enjoyment of all. But when you lay out flower beds or arrange areas for relaxing or playing consider adding the shapes of heaven and earth for balance. For instance, you might place round flower beds with square stepping stones or have square vegetable patches interspersed with round patches of growing herbs in between. Place a garden seat—perhaps a bench, swing or chair—so that there is somewhere to sit and enjoy mother nature.

Rule #3: If you or the people in your household have little or no time for garden work, the back yard is your last priority. Save any little time you do have for gardening in the front yard. A neat and tidy front yard will help attract positive and beneficial *Qi*, keeping both you and the neighbors happy.

The Front Porch and Door

Qi comes to all of us from the combination of the forces of heaven and earth. It travels through the countryside along the pathways and roads and on into the villages, towns and cities of our modern world. *Qi* then finds its way to your neighborhood and street. Now we simply need to apply good Feng Shui principles to make sure it finds your door.

Qi is usually drawn to the front door of a home. Now, many people tell me they never use their front door and that no one else ever does either and some people tell me they have two front doors, or that they use their attached garage or a side door between their garage and their homes as their main entrance. (Example: One client I saw recently at her beautiful Colonial home with an impressive center–front–entrance overlooking the river, invited me to enter her home through the garage door.)

Rule #1: When opportunity knocks, it always knocks at the front door. The side door, back door and garage door represent opportunities you are already expecting, promotions you should already have received, words of love from the spouse who is already your life partner, a tax refund you expect based on previous years' taxes—all things that are already yours. So, when we use Feng Shui to enhance the flow of *Qi*, we call or invite all of the new, unexpected, wonderful opportunities to come into our lives right through the front door. With this in mind, it would be nice if you, the resident, would use your front door occasionally. At least once a week, poke your head out the front door to check the flowers, the walkway, or to see whether the mail carrier left a package. This will help stir up the life force *Qi* trying to reach you.

Example: I was called to visit a pretty Cape Cod home because the owner and her husband were having trouble finding work. I rang the front bell and the owner shouted through the mail slot that I should enter around back. The woman said the front door lock had been broken and the door had been painted shut since they moved in a few months ago. I had her call the landlord to have the door fixed. She called me within just a few weeks to say that she and her husband were both happily employed.

Most houses have a front door that is both visible and accessible, although some houses do not. (Example: I recently was called to visit a bungalow–style home with a huge, gorgeous, wrap–around farmer's porch, but no front door. I had to walk around to the side of the house to find the entrance.) One cannot receive the positive benefits of *Qi*, if it cannot find a way in.

Cure: If the front door or main entrance of your residence is on one side of the house or, if your front door is inaccessible because of a gate, fence, or you have a Doberman in the front yard, or if the location of your front door is simply confusing (common for houses built on a corner lot), *Qi* will be confused about where to enter as well. Make the front door stand out. Create such a clear walkway leading to the front door that no visitor could mistake it. Ask friends and family members to help you out by using your front door instead of the alternative entrance(s). This will bring new *Qi*, new life force into your home (and into your world in general).

Rule #2: Make sure that the Qi feels welcome when it gets there.
When people do get to your front door, make sure they are greeted by a welcome mat. I have personally visited many fabulous homes filled with beautiful antiques, sumptuous furnishings and incredible pieces of art, but some owners scrimp on the all–important welcome mat. (Example: The mansard Victorian home filled with priceless antique Asian furniture and a torn–purple–towel–welcome–mat comes to mind...) Here are some suggestions for appropriate welcome mats:

1. A plain, high quality mat is fine. Choose the type that traps the dirt, keeping it out of your house. The best choice is a neutral color or black; rectangle or fan shapes are both good.

2. If you choose a colored mat, select a color that harmonizes with the type of Qi you are trying to attract. Red mats invite activity, an abundant flow of positive energy and good decision–making ability. Blue mats invite harmony into the dwelling. Yellow mats encourage friendships and social activities. Green mats call in prosperity. Black is the color of protection and privacy.

3. If you like mats with a design, choose a "friendly–looking" motif. (A cartoon character screaming "Get out!!!" is just bad Feng Shui!)

4. Mats are meant to be walked on, so avoid mats that display the family name, kittens or puppies or the American flag. None of these things are meant to be tread upon.

Rule #3: To precisely attract the energy you want, place a symbol of that energy on your front porch. Wind chimes, fountains, chairs, potted plants, sculptures or other artwork liven up a porch and therefore attract Qi. Here are some guidelines for decorating your porch:

Remove any damaged or broken artwork, furniture or decorations. Broken chimes do not attract harmonious Qi, broken chairs do not allow anyone to sit, plants in broken pots do not thrive. None of these will attract the type of Qi you want to welcome into your life.

Select objects that are in harmony with the type of Qi you are trying to attract. I know I sound like a "broken record," but this is one of the most important factors in achieving positive results from the application of Feng Shui. For example, if you want to enjoy more time resting and relaxing in your home–place a rocking chair on your porch. If you want more money Qi, hang a wind chime with gold–colored rods because the color gold attracts the energy of large sums of money. And, if you are afraid of snakes and wish to attract warm, fuzzy, bunny Qi (for fertility or new love) to your home—whatever you do, do not hang a nine–foot metal snake on one of the pillars of the porch. (Yes, I have seen one.)

Choose objects that are in proportion to the size of your porch. There needs to be enough room for people to approach your front door without tripping over plants or banging their heads into a chime. If you have a small porch then keep it largely unadorned; if you have a large porch, decorate away. (Example: I saw one porch that was too small for any furniture, and the owner had painted a mural of a chair and a table with flowers. It was a very good idea, made a most pleasant impression and had attracted a lot of good *Qi* into his life.)

If there is an enclosed porch, it can be decorated in much the same way a room in the house might be done—using weather-resistant furniture, if appropriate. If you have an enclosed porch, please don't make it a "dumping ground" for all of your odds and ends. Even though the clutter cannot be seen from the street, it is seen by everyone who enters your home. The clutter sets the tone for all the *Qi* that enters as well. If you do have an enclosed porch, make it clear to the visitor whether they should go through to the door of the house or if they should make their presence known from the porch door.

Light attracts *Qi*. Keep your porch light in good working order. Always replace a burned out bulb with one equally as bright.

Chapter 4

Feng Shui and Your Home's Public Spaces

Knock, knock! Who's there? It's *Qi*, finally. The *Qi* has at last found its way to your front door and is about to enter your home. Let us welcome it inside. There are any number of floor plans for the houses we live in. Some people have a specified entryway, foyer, indoor landing, etc., others have front doors that open directly into a room. Entryways provide the transition point for people to come in from outside and become accustomed to the change in the level of light, difference of temperature and shift in mood. So, if I should drop by your house for a surprise visit, and you open the front door, what, besides you standing there holding the door, would I see?

Entryways

First, let us consider formal entryways. If you do not have one of these, you may want to skip to the section on Living Rooms (pp. 63). Even if you are a very casual person by nature, your entryway should be a bit more formal and a touch more impressive than other rooms of the house. Like energy attracts like. (This is the concept that similar energies are attracted to each other, we tend to like people who are like us and people who have money seem to get more money and so on.) And a grand entry will attract grand opportunities. However, grand or not, here are a few important considerations:

Rule #1: The entryway should not be dark. A dark entryway will not attract good *Qi*. Natural light is best, so having windows near the front door, or having a front door with glass panes in it will attract better opportunities to everyone living in the house.

Cure: Indoor lighting is one way to go if there are no windows in your entryway or front door. Use bright lighting. During the daytime, the contrast between the bright outside and a dim entryway may cause guests to stumble. And at night, it is very pleasant for your guests (and for you and other family members)

Entryways

Fig. 9: A closed in entryway can cause a person entering to feel tired, rundown and apathetic. Solution: paint the close wall a cheerful color or hang art that is lively, and fun.

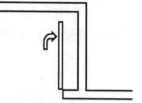

Fig. 10: A blocked doorway means guests and Qi will have to squeeze in the door. This will limit career and relationship opportunities for all in the house. Solution: remove extra furniture and let the door swing open freely.

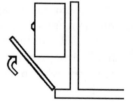

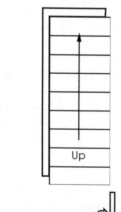

Up

Fig. 11: A particularly difficult situation is when the stairs face the main door. This allows all the Qi the family has worked so hard to attract to run right back out the door causing opportunities to slip away. Solution: hang a decorative mirror above the door facing into the house. The mirror can be quite small, less than four inches, and it can be incorporated into a piece of art, silk plant arrangement or wall design. It is most effective when it looks like it belongs there.

Main Door

to enter a bright, warm, welcoming space as they come into the residence.

Rule #2: The entry should not feel too closed in (see fig. 9). Sometimes the space reserved for the entryway is too small, usually one has been carved out of available square footage by building a close–in wall to separate the living area from the door. If a door opens directly into a wall, furniture or clutter, every visitor will feel a choked or tight sensation immediately upon entering the home (see fig. 10). Needless to say, *Qi* will not easily find its way into the rest of the home. As for you, however excited you may feel about coming home at the end of your day, however many enthusiastic plans you may have for enjoying your evening, the minute you open your door upon that close–in wall, all of your enthusiasm drains away, and it takes every bit of your remaining strength to simply get inside and find a chair to sit down on.

Rule #3: The height of the door defines the minimum distance to the opposing wall. In other words, if the door were to fall inward, would it hit the opposing wall? If it would, then you have a close–in wall.

Cure: If the area cannot be opened up architecturally you will need to place something in the area to make the space feel more open. If the opposing wall is actually a full wall and not a closet door, for instance, you could hang a picture or painting on it. Select a wide open landscape scene or a bright floral. Whenever someone enters the house through your front door, they will be greeted by a pleasant vista or a cheerful scene that distracts them from the stifled closed in feeling. You could choose pictures that have a personal meaning for you, as long as they represent the types of things you would like to attract into your life. Do not place a mirror in this instance, as mirrors reflect *Qi* back in the opposite direction. The mirror reflects the open door, sending the *Qi* back out through the door before it can make its way into the rest of the house. If you would like to hang a mirror in the entryway, you may do so, but be sure to hang it in such a way that any entering *Qi* is reflected into your home.

If there is a closet door immediately opposite your entrance door, it might look odd to hang a picture on it. Consider painting the closet door an attractive and even surprising or unusual color; or consider a high–gloss paint to make the closet door really glow.

You might even consider painting a pattern on your closet door. Be creative and try something out of the ordinary—after all, you can always repaint.

Example: One of my clients has a louvered closet door immediately opposite her narrow entrance doorway. She painted the louvers in a variety of pastel shades and made a quite plain and ill–placed closet door into a piece of art much admired by all who visit her home.

Rule #4: Half walls need special consideration. Half walls cut entering Qi in two. There are two types of half walls. One is the wall that does not extend from floor to ceiling but allows a person to look over it and on into the home. This is sometimes called a "pony wall." The other type of half wall extends from floor to ceiling, but it blocks half of your view into the room beyond.

Half walls allow your eyes to move forward into the space beyond but not your feet. In order to get into the next room, you must navigate around the wall. The same thing is required of the entering Qi. It must find its way around the half wall and on into the rest of the house. Unfortunately, it is not always that easy to persuade Qi to make a turn! Qi travels like a river but it is greatly slowed by obstacles like walls. A wall such as this divides the Qi and can cause a scattering of the overall flow of energy into the home.

Cure: If you cannot remove the half wall that divides your entrance area from the rest of your home, place plants on the pony wall. Select the kind of plant that has tendrils that can drape over the wall. This will provide the entering Qi with a little "ladder" to help it get up and over or around the half wall.

If your half wall is of the variety that divides your view vertically, half of the entering Qi will move on into the rooms, and half will be blocked by the wall itself. Split Qi is very unsettling. People living in the home usually start many projects and then have problems finishing them, or they may have a great deal of difficulty making choices and decisions.

Cure: For vertical half walls hang a piece of art on the wall, anything that is pleasant or attractive will do. Then your eyes will choose either to focus on the artwork or on the room ahead. Upon entering the home, the positive Qi will encourage the residents and guests to find the energy to complete projects as well as make clear decisions concerning any future course of action.

Rule #5: An ascending staircase should not face the entryway. Often times in Colonial or Cape–style houses the first thing we see when the front door is opened is a staircase leading up. All of the *Qi* you worked so hard to bring to the front door of the home enters the house and immediately "hits" the staircase (see fig. 11). It takes great effort for the *Qi* to move up the staircase. Often it can't make it all the way up and it turns and runs back down and out the door. If the staircase is to one side of the door, *Qi* will not flow directly out the door. It is only when the bottom stair of a staircase lines up with the door that the *Qi* escapes as quickly as it enters the home. The closer the staircase is to the door, the greater the problem. If the staircase faces a door but it is 15 feet or more away, there may be no problem. However, if the staircase is closer than the measured height of the door (in other words, less than six feet away) *Qi* is being lost. The way this type of problem expresses itself in the lives of the people who live in the home is that promised opportunities never materialize, everything takes more effort than it should and good luck seems fleeting.

   Cure: We must stop the *Qi* from flowing out through the front door as quickly as it enters. Here are several cures that can work in this type of situation:

1. If there is enough floor space in the entryway, place a living plant between the door and the staircase. If the stairs are wide enough, place small plants at the corner of the stairs—being careful not to crowd the stairway. It is sufficiently difficult to encourage the *Qi* to move up a staircase, and we don't want to block or "choke" the flow in any way.

2. Hang a crystal from the chandelier in the entryway. This works best if the crystal blends in with the existing light fixture. If there already is a crystal chandelier in the entryway, that is good news. Otherwise, consider hanging a small round prismatic crystal from the existing light fixture. *Qi* will bounce off the crystal and move into the house in small rainbows of light.

3. If there is no light fixture or the ceiling is too high, then consider placing a mirror (not the Feng Shui protection mirror mentioned previously) above the front door, facing the staircase. Choose a

decorative mirror in a size proportional to the space above the door. The mirror itself should be small, five inches in diameter or less. A good selection is a small mirror forming part of a piece of wall art, for example, one that is in the center of a wreath or part of a plaque.

At the beginning of this chapter I asked what I might see immediately inside your front door if I were to pay a surprise visit to your home. Let us now take a look at the colors and the décor of your entryway, and see if your current choices are attracting the type of Qi that can best benefit your life.

If I were to give you a list of life benefits and ask you to choose from such things as: happy career, abundant wealth, loving relationships, happy family, successful children, respected wisdom, caring friends, physical health, safety and security, inner joy and peace—which would you pick? You may say that you want it all, and that's fine—but it will be a little crowded in your entryway. Consider choosing one of these for your focus at this time. Select one that is really meaningful and important to you now, something that would make your effort to attain the others easier.

For instance, you might say, "If I had a great relationship with my family, this would help my children, relieve a lot of my personal stress issues (thus improving my health), and allow me to focus more energy on my career." Or, you might say, "If I could find a career that I felt excited about, and if I both loved doing my job and received recognition for my efforts, then everything else would fall into place. I would have time for friends, time for study, time for investing and time to take care of my health." Or, you might tell me, "If I enjoyed good health I could feel satisfaction and joy in every other aspect of my life," or, "If I just had enough money, then everything else would fall into place…"

When working with Feng Shui to improve the flow of energy in your home and in your lives, in general we want to take a holistic approach. To do this, we will address our attention to each and every room of the house. However, at this point, we are concentrating on the main theme—the leading issue in your life right now is the best and most important focus for the fresh Qi coming into your house, for the new energy finding its way into your life.

Here are some specific cures to place in the entryway to help focus the *Qi* as it enters your home:

Health: Choose living plants (especially herbs), pictures of lush and growing life, traditional symbols of health (such as the caduceus) or books on healthful living. Choose any shade of green, as this is the color that represents health and well–being. Remove any bones, images of dead things, dried flowers, pictures of barren landscapes. Remove anything that might distract you from your health goals (like that candy dish on the entrance table...)

Wealth: Choose living plants with round leaves (a money plant—lunaria annua—is an excellent choice), a brass bowl (to catch the money coming into the home), decorations with coins (see Coin Charms, pp. 217), pictures of flowing water, waterfalls or ocean waves. Find a place near your entryway to display objects that have value to you: statues, art, collectibles. Use the colors green, purple, burgundy or gold in your décor. Remove any catalogs, bills, cheap knickknacks and anything plastic from the entryway as this distracts the wealth *Qi*.

Relationships: Choose pairs of things (birds, bunnies, dogs, hearts, flowers, herbs) as you decorate your entrance area. Hang pictures showing people holding hands, walking on the beach— any picture that suggests romance. Choose the colors red, pink, peach and orange as you detail your décor. Remove single objects, pictures of past loves (unless you want them to come back into your life), single subject pictures, and cats (stuffed, statues or pictures); they are too independent to represent the desire to attract a relationship...don't worry, we will find another place for them. Remove protection symbols, anything sharp or pointy, weapons and protection mirrors.

Wisdom: Choose pictures of a spiritual nature, or of spiritual masters. Choose ones that mean something to you personally and spiritually. Place books and study materials here; you may also place study equipment in the area. (Some people might place a magnifying glass, scales, a telescope for viewing the heavens or a microscope... A pharmacist might have a mortar and pestle, an interior designer may have framed house plans, a person on a spiritual quest may have a stone from a sacred place, etc.) Choose shades of purple, blue or gray for your color scheme. Remove electronics, televisions (though I doubt you have one in the entryway), video games and any half–finished projects.

Family Harmony: Select pictures of family members and hang them in wooden frames in the entrance area. Place mementos of family history (like photo albums) in the space; combine personal treasures among the things that once belonged to other family members. Grow a small tree here (to represent the "family tree"). Choose shades of the colors green and brown as you decorate. Remove weapons, sharp objects and anything made of metal.

Children's Success: Hang or place pictures of children playing, pictures of your own children, toys and other bright, colorful or playful items in the area. Add the color white. Store school books here, display diplomas and awards. Remove clocks, calendars, plants and weapons.

Happy Career: Hang awards, certificates and diplomas in the entrance area. Place a clock or calendar where it is easy to see. Add the colors black and blue to your décor and add a fountain. Remove toys, books and other articles related to your former studies (you are fully trained now) and any book bags or school paraphernalia.

Caring Friends: Place or hang pictures of friends, gifts from friends and awards received for charitable work done. Add the color yellow to the décor and some flowering plants.

Protection and Safety: Place sharp, pointy objects on several surfaces (or hang them on the wall); protection mirrors or protection charms (see the section on Mirrors on pp. 147) are also good choices for the entrance area. Display cacti or plants with sharp leaves or thorns. Place a "guardian," an animal, angel or ancestor symbol, facing the door to watch what enters. Paint the door blue (it is said that an evil spirit cannot pass through a blue door). Hang bells on the door—their sound will chase away any evil spirits that have attached themselves to your visitors. Remove stuffed animals and any pillows, quilts or doilies.

Inner Joy: Hang pictures of flowers or place cut flowers in the entrance area. Choose pictures of wonderful places and beautiful, peaceful scenes. Or, hang pictures of happy people enjoying a party or celebration. Remove anything that is depressing (bills, muddy boots, pictures of people you are not fond of, etc.). Ask yourself if you feel obligated to have a particular item in that space. If the answer is "yes," remove it and replace it with something you want to have in the entrance area.

Alternative Entryways

If you regularly enter your home through a side door or a garage door, yet have the option of using the front door—please, at least once a week, use the main door. Invite guests to visit, greet the parcel delivery person or use the door yourself as much as possible. This will help stimulate new opportunities.

Rule #4: Your side door or garage door is not the ideal entry. Most alternative doorways lead directly into a space that is usually cluttered, dark, unattractive and sometimes cramped. When you enter through an alternative doorway (one that is not the main entrance or front door of the house) the first thing you are likely to see is the garage, or laundry room. However, people often tell me that it is much more convenient to use the alternative entryway than the front entrance to their home. But no one wants to be greeted by a pile of unfinished laundry or dirty dishes in the sink upon coming home. Here are some ideas for those of you who need to use an alternative entry to get into your home.

Cure: Make the area bright. Bright is at least cheerful and so if you have to enter a small, cramped area—at least arrange for a welcoming light to greet you. Consider also painting the area a cheerful color. Keep the clutter to a minimum, and hang curtains or place a screen to block the view of unattractive areas. Have a rack for shoes, hang hooks for jackets, and keep stuff off the floors.

Think about the things you usually carry into the house when you return home and create places for those things. Find a good place for briefcases, the lunch box, the umbrella. If each item has a home it will help considerably to control the clutter. Make the alternative entryway as attractive as possible. If the first thing you see is the washer and dryer, hang an attractive curtain to hide them (or hang folding doors if there is enough room). Hang attractive pictures in your mud room or on an entryway wall. If you enter your home through a mudroom, make this space into a real living space, not simply a closet. Place a thick, washable rug on the floor in your alternative entryway to welcome your arrival home.

Living Room

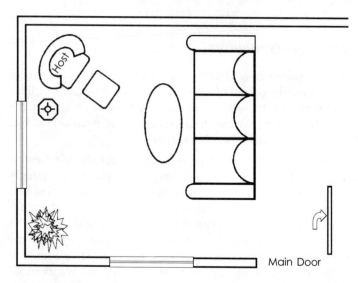

Main Door

Fig. 12: The host's chair should face the main entrance to the room. This is the power position and can be used whenever a person wants to have authority in a situation or feel in charge of their destiny.

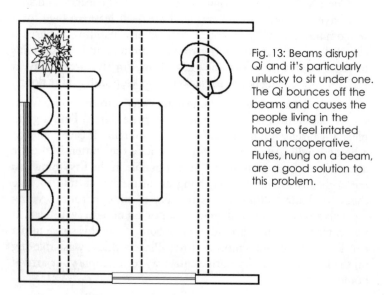

Fig. 13: Beams disrupt Qi and it's particularly unlucky to sit under one. The Qi bounces off the beams and causes the people living in the house to feel irritated and uncooperative. Flutes, hung on a beam, are a good solution to this problem.

Living Rooms

In the past the living room was one of the formal areas in a home. People mostly used this room to entertain and receive guests in their home. It was a public room, a picture–perfect representation of the homeowner's lifestyle, a symbol of their status in the community. Now, chances are that you either never use your living room or you use it for everything. At least, that is what statistics based on studies of typical American family practices tell us. Studies also suggest that you entertain guests less than four percent of the time you are at home. These studies tell us that the main function and purpose of the modern–day living room has changed greatly over the years. No matter, your living room has three main requirements: first, it needs to feel welcoming to the *Qi* entering your home; second, it needs to be comfortable for the family; third, it needs to provide a place to display the interests and goals of the family members.

Rule #1: Your living room should be welcoming. This means that it feels welcoming to you, your family, your guests and to *Qi*. Do not block doors. If there is a door you cannot fully open because a piece of furniture is in the way, *Qi* is blocked from entering (and leaving) the room as it flows through your home (see fig. 10). Many times people wait and wish for a new job, a new relationship or to feel more energetic or healthy. When *Qi* cannot easily enter the living room in their homes, people end up waiting for opportunities and benefits in their lives.

Cure: Move the furniture out of the way and let the *Qi* in. (This rule goes for all doors leading into the living room.)

Rule #2: Decorate to create a feeling of harmony. Your living room might never be displayed on the cover of a decorating magazine but it can be pleasant and comfortable. If you and other members of your family spend a lot of time in this room, then it is an important room in your lives and you deserve to enjoy good décor.

Cure: Matching shapes help create a visually harmonious décor. If several pieces of furniture repeat a similar basic shape (e.g., square, octagonal, round, oblong, etc.) the furniture will create the sense of harmony we are trying to establish in the living room. Even if the separate pieces do not match perfectly, some are older and some newer, together they will create a pleasing décor. On the other hand, if the coffee table is oval, an end table octagonal and another is square, there will be a feeling that something is incongruent and there might be a sense of disharmony in the space.

Try to keep pieces of furniture in proportion with the size of the living room and with one another. Also, a room filled with only upholstered pieces would feel unbalanced. Keep Yin (upholstered) pieces in proportion with Yang (wooden) furniture pieces. If the living room is small use fewer pieces of furniture rather than numerous smaller pieces. If the room is large, group pieces into several different seating arrangements.

The seating depth of the sofa should match the depth of the chairs—unless there are great height differences in the members of the family. Furniture doesn't have to match to feel coordinated. If the end tables are made of wood that does not match, for instance, you can still match them in height (within one inch) and they will look great together.

Large pieces of artwork, paintings or pictures, should be placed or hung at eye level, usually about sixty inches from the floor to the center of the piece. Mirrors can also serve as artwork; they add light and depth to a room. Smaller mirrors can be hung as decoration, at any level but larger mirrors should be hung like art, at eye level. Mirrors should not be placed facing the main entrance to the living room unless they are on a wall at least fifteen feet from the entrance to the room. In general, mirrors facing an entrance send the *Qi* back outside the room. If a mirror is large enough to reflect a person's head it needs to be set at a height that allows the tallest member of the family to see his or her whole head.—cutting off someone's head is considered bad for their health. (See Chapter 9, Mirrors, pp. 147 for more information.)

Choose a focal point for your living room. Perhaps there is a fireplace or a picture window. If there is no natural focal point, hang a piece of art and build around that. This will give the living room an "anchor" and create a sense of harmony and unity within the home.

That being said, have only one focal point. If there is both a fireplace and a television in the living room you potentially have two focal points. Mask one to balance the room (ideally, tuck the television away in a cabinet). Too many focal points create a distraction, resulting in the people in the home feeling scattered and unfocused in their lives. The scattered *Qi* resulting from this type of décor makes it difficult for the residents to accomplish tasks easily or to reach their goals.

Rule #3: Furniture should be placed to allow Qi to flow easily through the space. Think of *Qi* as if it were a river of gold flowing through your living room. This river will tend to move straight through the room from one end to the other unless something causes it to shift its course. A gentle change of direction is the most beneficial. Imagine this river slowing slightly, symbolically dropping its gold throughout the room. However, we do not want to stop the flow by cutting off sections of the room from positive *Qi*, nor do we want to cause this river to make sharp, unnatural turns. Think gentle curves for a meandering river of gold as you place your furnishings harmoniously in your living room.

Avoid hanging too many protection mirrors, placing too many guardian statues or displaying weapons. It is especially important not to over–protect the living room if you have a business in the home, or if you are trying to sell the house. Usually one or two protection symbols in a room are sufficient. (And remove them entirely if the home is for sale.) Placing too many protection symbols in the living room has the same effect as if you created walls of protection on all four sides. While this may sound very safe, nothing can enter a solid cube—no energy, no income, no relationships, no happiness, no *Qi*.

The second important purpose of the living room is to provide a place of comfort and relaxation for all who live in the home. Whether you have a second living area or not, the living room needs to live up to its name: it needs to be a place where living happens. If you have a "great room," this can be the formal space in the home, the area with the white carpeting and hard and uncomfortable furnishings that keep people from sitting (or staying) very long. But your living room needs to be lived in.

Place a chair or sofa where you would like to sit when you are alone in the room. Sit in the chair and look around the room. Imagine guests there and anticipate where they would sit and how they would interact with you and each other. Are they at a comfortable distance for carrying on a conversation? Is it easy for them to place a drink or a snack nearby?

Picture yourself sharing the room with the other members of your family, everyone talking and laughing and enjoying one another's company. Have they all found a comfortable place to sit? Does everyone feel they can connect easily with one another? Is there room for family pets to move around easily?

Finally, picture the room just as it is now, just you, sitting in a chair. Maybe you have just set down a good book next to your cup of coffee or tea. How does it feel to be in this room, just you, by yourself? Is the chair comfortable and inviting? Is there a place to put your feet up? Is it quiet enough?

Rule #4: Your living room should be a showcase for you and your family's personality and the family's hopes for the future. This will create what is called a spirit hearth, a spiritual and personal center for the home. A spirit hearth consists often of a symbol or group of symbols that tell the story of who you are (as a family) and where you are going in your life/lives. In times past, such a symbol might have been a coat of arms or a religious altar. Today it may be a table that holds objects that have a particular meaning to the members of your family; it might be a wall of pictures, a collection of things you cherish and things that inspire you.

Example: In one song writer's home, a round table in the living room displayed a valuable old photograph of a man playing the piano. A few sheets of original music were placed on the table and a beautiful, expensive guitar leaned against it. In another home, the family had a small rectangular table covered in a white embroidered cloth. A statue of the Hindu God Ganesh was placed on the table, surrounded by flowers and candles. A third home had a wall in the living room dotted with pictures of grandchildren and, in the center of the same wall, an alabaster plaque of an angel.

As you create your own spirit hearth, be sure to clear out any clutter in the room. The living room represents the way you see yourself, it stands for who you are—not who you have been in the past. Make sure that your room is not filled with everything that has been accumulated over the years. Some possessions may have sentimental value to you, but if the collection cannot be displayed in a balanced and harmonious way, then you are neither honoring yourself nor the memories you treasure. Clear the clutter.

Choose items that honor your past. These may be pictures of your ancestors, a memento from childhood or a symbol of where you came from. Some people place religious symbols or paintings of a childhood home. Some place a special piece of furniture from their ancestral home. I, for instance, have chosen to display a hand–tooled leather box from my grandfather's collection in my living room.

Having selected some memento of the past to display in your living room, now place something in the room that symbolizes your goals for the future. What is your goal? Is it to have a family you are proud of, to enjoy a loving relationship with your partner, great health, riches, achievement?

Example: One client loves information and makes every effort to always be well–informed. He would like others to see him as a source of answers and solutions. My suggestion to him was to create a spirit hearth in his living room filled with books—old books, new books and books he particularly treasures. This is a symbol for one of his most important goals, a future filled with stimulating conversation and exchange of ideas and concepts. As you arrange your living room, allow each member of your family to place some symbol of their goals and wishes for the future in the space.

Here are some basic Feng Shui rules for furniture placement in living rooms:

When seated, the host should be able to view the entrance to the room (see fig. 12). It is your house, and you should sit in the most powerful position in the living room; that would be the chair facing the main door/entrance to the room. It is quite acceptable for guests to sit with their backs to the door. Even though some people find this position quite uncomfortable, it is preferable to seat a guest in this way, as they are less likely to stay in the house a long period of time, unlike the host or hostess who live in the home.

Heavy ceiling beams can be an issue in some homes. In general, the rules of Feng Shui dictate that exposed beams disrupt Qi, causing the people who live under them to feel overwhelmed or over–burdened in life. With this in mind, I always suggest that people not place chairs and sofas directly under beams in their living rooms (see fig. 13). Overhead soffits, when used to cover interior structural beams or heating/cooling ducts, will not have the same effect as exposed beams if they are painted the same color as the ceiling. Vigas—the log–cabin–type logs that are sometimes used as beams—are round but still affect Qi very much the same way rectangular beams do. Make sure to place chairs and sofas so that they are not directly under beams. (See Flutes, pp. 165.)

Large pieces of furniture with sharp, protruding corners can create poison arrows. Examples of this problem can be seen with Chippendale–, Colonial– and Victorian–style furniture. If the corners of a prominent piece of furniture in the living room protrudes like a dart, it can slice the room's energy and create discord in the home. The problem is particularly apparent when the piece faces an entryway or a seating area, however, if it faces a window or fireplace there is no need to adjust the placement of the piece in the room. If it is not possible to relocate the piece, cover the protruding corner with a cloth or a plant with draping vines; or, place a large plant between the piece of furniture and the seating area at which it points.

Whenever possible, keep the television hidden from view when it is not in use. This may not be easy (depending on the size of your television) but it is better for the Qi if this is kept hidden. There is a happy trend now among manufacturers, making some of today's televisions look more like a piece of art hanging on the wall; there are even some models that look liked framed mirrors. If possible, choose one of these when you make your next selection. Or, choose a cabinet with doors which can be shut when the television is not in use.

If you have a very large living room, instead of placing a few pieces of furniture along the walls and at a distance from one another, create several inviting seating areas in the space. Furniture spread too far apart keeps others "at arm's length" and does not allow close friendships and relationships to develop.

When your living room needs to be used for multiple purposes, organize your furniture so that the various activities do not impose on one another.

Example: One client used her living room both for entertaining and as a home office. I advised her to separate the two functions by using a folding screen to divide the space. She affirms that now, when her workday is done, she can relax without thinking about tasks that are not yet completed. And, during the workday, she finds herself much less distracted by the people and activities that used to disturb her concentration.

Chapter 5

Feng Shui and
Your Home's Private Spaces

Kitchens

The kitchen is the heart of the home. It is where family and friends gather—and where *Qi* can accumulate. Contrary to the way life was lived in the past, we live in an age where the amount of time available to us for spending with our loved ones is limited due to our hectic lifestyles. We are likely to find less and less time to actually cook a meal or sit down with our family to eat. This is a shame because it was mealtime that would bring families together to talk and share their experiences with one another each day. Children would learn about their parents' lives and parents could hear about the successes and the struggles their children faced during their days.

We can still enhance the feeling of closeness with family members by having a kitchen that encourages everyone to feel comfortable. When we love to be in a space it becomes more fun to spend time there. So, activities that take place in the space move up on our list of priorities and suddenly we find more time to spend enjoying the space and time to share with one another. When we are comfortable in a space, we welcome others to join us and soon sharing and connecting are part of our lives once more.

The kitchen is considered the "heart of the home" in Feng Shui because it is the room where all five of the Chinese elements are naturally represented in the environment. There is wood in the cabinets, water flows from the faucets in the sink, fire is represented by the stove, the appliances (and pots and pans) are constructed of metal and the floor represents earth (as well, counters may be formed from granite or other earthy materials). With all five elements present, a balance unlike that of any other room in the house is maintained. *Qi* circulates freely, and attracts even more energy. People are drawn to the powerful *Qi* in the space—that is why everyone always seems find their way to the kitchen, and to stay there as long as possible.

If you don't like your kitchen, it can feel as if the whole house is out of balance. You will not want to spend time there, creating meals becomes a chore, cleaning up after becomes a burden and clutter accumulates on every surface. If the kitchen is not comfortable for you, then the very essence of the house feels "out of whack." Righting a kitchen should be your first priority, for when the kitchen Qi is balanced, you will attract the energy and resources to make changes in the rest of the house. Maybe you have paged through those decorating magazines more than a few times and admired the pristine, perfect kitchens, whether the ultra–modern all stainless steel or an old–world, Mediterranean style with stone and wood. Maybe you have admired a modern version of a 1950's kitchen, or perhaps you wish for new cabinets, new floors, new appliances and new countertops (and maybe a skylight would be nice as well). And possibly all of this is not in your current budget. So, let's think about what can be done right now.

The first lesson of Feng Shui is to create a place where you love to spend time. So, think back to a good experience you had in a kitchen. It may not have been your family kitchen, it could have been your grandmother's or your aunt's—perhaps it was a friend's kitchen. Picture yourself in that kitchen and ask yourself why the experience was good. "Who was there?" "What was the occasion?" "What was being prepared?" "What was your role in the preparations?" Finally, ask yourself, "What about that kitchen lent itself to this good time I had?"

Example: I remember my grandma's when we visited for Sunday dinner. It was a plain, galley–style kitchen with original 1938 cabinets and a 1939 GE refrigerator with a tiny, little icebox freezer. There was a huge sink, big enough to bathe a child in, and I remember Grandpa standing over the sink, washing the dishes. But the thing I remember most was that Grandma had a chair over by the stove where she could sit and talk while watching the pots to keep them from boiling over. Now my current kitchen, with its modern light pine cabinets and stainless steel appliances, the walls painted brightly in melon and sky blue, is very unlike my grandma's kitchen—at least in appearance. But in this kitchen I have a chair where I can sit and watch the stove, just like my grandma would have done. And this one aspect makes it comfortable for me.

Kitchens

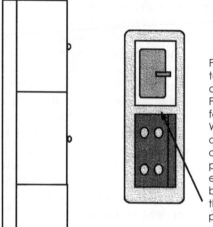

Fig. 14: The cooktop and sink together on an island create a conflict of fire and water. Fire brings action to the family, water brings emotion. When these two elements are in conflict impulsive action can overwhelm people's feelings and intense emotions can create erratic behavior. Solution: separate the two elements with a plant or wood divider.

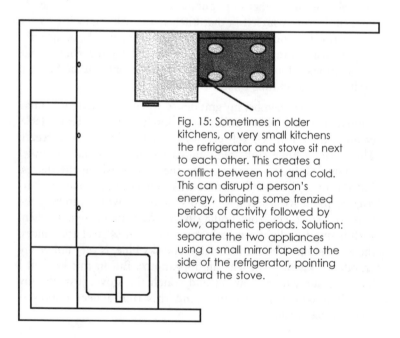

Fig. 15: Sometimes in older kitchens, or very small kitchens the refrigerator and stove sit next to each other. This creates a conflict between hot and cold. This can disrupt a person's energy, bringing some frenzied periods of activity followed by slow, apathetic periods. Solution: separate the two appliances using a small mirror taped to the side of the refrigerator, pointing toward the stove.

Consider your answers to the questions above and find one aspect of a past that you can apply to your current place. It might be the way the pots were hung, or a row of spices displayed in unique bottles; maybe it was a small section of a counter used for journaling; or, a window sill with herbs and flowers in little pots. Add this comfortable aspect to your kitchen and you will change its energy immediately.

Back from memory lane and on to the Feng Shui rules. Here are some guidelines for your kitchen:

Rule #1: A kitchen should not be next to a bathroom. In other words, if a single door in the kitchen leads directly into a bathroom, it is too close. This is quite a common design because it is so much cheaper to build a bathroom where there is already plumbing for a kitchen. But the bathroom with its particular *Qi* is not really an appropriate neighbor for a kitchen.

Cure: Keep the bathroom door closed at all times. Keep the toilet seat down. For added protection, hang a mirror above the door in the bathroom, pointing back into the bathroom. In this case the mirror should be small (even one inch across is sufficient) and it can be a part of some floral decoration or plaque above the door.

Rule #2: A single door should not lead directly from the kitchen into a bedroom. Usually this type of arrangement only occurs when a room like a study or garage has been converted into a bedroom. It is considered bad for the health to have a person sleep next to a room where steam, grease and smoke from the day's cooking can move easily from one room to another.

Cure: Even if you have a smoke–free, grease–free, steam–free kitchen, it is best to keep the bedroom door closed at all times. Add plants to the bedroom to protect the health of the person/ people who sleep there.

Rule #3: It should not be possible to see the kitchen from the entrance to the home. This is a very common layout in small apartments and condos. One enters the home through the front door and the kitchen is immediately to either the right or left. Feng Shui lore says that if the kitchen can be viewed from the front door, you will end up feeding and taking care of everyone.

Cure: If someone entering your home can easily see your kitchen, and if you already have a problem with setting boundaries (and you are aware that other people take advantage of your good-heartedness), then place a "guardian" at the entrance to your kitchen pointing toward the door. Guardians can be spiritual statues, animals or plants with sharp points (like aloe vera). Another solution, is to hang a short curtain from the top of the door that extends down to the level of the average adult's chin. This obscures the view into the kitchen without closing off the energy. And still another solution is to hang a wind chime at the entrance to the kitchen. Hang it high enough so that no one bumps their head on it when entering the kitchen. Make sure to choose one that chimes sweetly, this way your guests will only have sweet things to say about you and you will not feel obligated to give them all of your resources, your time and your energy, just to keep the peace.

Now, let us continue into the kitchen and begin by examining the stove. The stove is the center of fire, "the hearth" of your kitchen.

Rule #4: Since the stove represents the fire element, it should not be adjacent to objects that represent the water element. Sinks and refrigerators represent the water element. There should always be a bit of counter space between the stove and sink (see fig. 14), and the stove and refrigerator (see fig. 15). Combining these two elements can cause fiery arguments on the one hand and drowning of energy on the other.

Cure: If there is no counter space, then there will be a gap. Place a mirror on the side of the stove pointing toward the refrigerator or sink. The mirror can be quite small, even less than two inches in diameter, and can be affixed with tape or glue. This mirror will reflect the discordant energy back to the refrigerator or sink and help separate the two conflicting elements.

Rule #5: When you stand facing the stove, you should not have your back to any door. Often this is complicated because a kitchen can have more than one entrance. But it is quite uncomfortable to cook standing with your back to the door; the likely result is that you will avoid cooking in your kitchen, and the health of your family could suffer.

Cure: The solution is to put something above the stove that will reflect what is behind you. The mirror is often suggested as a cure and though mirrors are very effective in reflecting Qi, it may not be an aesthetically pleasing option in your kitchen. Consider attaching a piece of Plexiglas behind the stove. This will not only protect the wall from splashes but it will reflect behind you as well. If you have tile as a backsplash, it may already provide a reflective surface. Other reflective surfaces that go well behind a stove are a decorative plate, a clock, or a hanging pot. A range hood can also be a reflective surface. Finally, one added benefit to reflecting the surface behind the stove, according to Feng Shui lore, is that increasing the number of burners in appearance (so what was four, now appears to be six or eight) is said to increase the amount of money you attract.

Rule #6: The stove should not be placed under a window. This is quite rare and I have only seen this placement in very old houses. Chinese lore says that a window over the stove means that food on the stove will go bad and so will the family's financial luck.

   Cure: If you have a window over your stove, consider hanging black–out shades behind your curtains, or hang shutters instead of curtains.

Rule #7: Keep faucets in good repair. A leaky faucet can mean your money is leaking away.

   Cure: Repair faucets to keep yourself from being nickel and dimed to death.

Rule #8: Keep drains free of clogs. A clogged drain can mean there is no monetary flow in your life. It is sometimes suggested that you plug or close all of your drains to cure the problem. This is not true. It is fine to leave your drains open—for whatever is going to go down the drain is not something you wanted to keep. To have true flow, some money must go out as part of the cycle. (We just want to make sure that more comes in than goes out.) Keep drains free of clogs and money will flow.

Rule #9: Decorate the kitchen in a color in harmony with the energy you want to attract.

   Cure: Kitchens that are black and white bring a no–nonsense feel into the space, kitchen work is done with speed and efficiency. Kitchens that are just white can feel very clean but they can also can feel sterile. The yellow kitchen evokes happy memories of times spent in family kitchens; it is a good choice for someone who wants to get back to the basics in cooking. Greens, including mint, sage

Dining Room Tables

The dining room table can be many styles and shapes. First and foremost it needs to be stable, not rocking back and forth on uneven legs. A rocking table would bring instability to the family.

Square and Rectangular tables represent the element of earth and bring additional stability to the family.

Round and oval tables represent heaven and bring a sense of harmony and balance.

Octagonal tables encompass the eight life stations, eight trigrams of the *I Ching*, the eight virtues, etc. The number eight is said to bring happiness because it looks like the Chinese word for happiness.

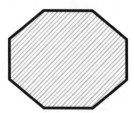

and forest greens, are the colors for growth and wellness. Choose shades of green for rugs, potholders and towels. Red will bring energy to the cooking and cleaning experience, but too much red may make you hurry too much. It may cause you to try to cook things too quickly, or to rush your meals. Blue represents the energy of heaven and can be very comforting in the kitchen, as long as the color does not appear too cold. The kitchen should be a place of warmth. The color purple is not one that supports the physicality of life; so a purple kitchen is more about a "look" and less about health. Pink is seldom a good choice, it tends to make the whole cooking experience very tiring. Tan kitchens encourage tidiness and a focus on the details. Orange kitchens support the digestive process, and peach kitchens bring creativity and fun to kitchen work. (See Chapter 15, Color, pp. 206, for more information.)

Example: In New Mexico I consulted for a woman who had no kitchen at all. After her bitter divorce she vowed she would "never cook for another man" and she had her kitchen removed.

There was literally no stove, no refrigerator and no sink in her home. I have heard about a trend in California to offer apartments for young executives with nothing more than a sink, a microwave and a small hotel refrigerator instead of a kitchen space. Houses like these have no heart, and the people who live in them will not connect with the house. Often housing for the elderly is set up with no kitchen, no heart and no expectancy that the occupant will stay long. Try always to live in a home with a kitchen. This will allow you to feel comfortable and at home in the house/ apartment until it is time for you to move on.

Note: In China, many homes have a small shrine to the "kitchen god" next to the stove. The kitchen god guards the kitchen, helping food to be cooked well and taste good. He listens to arguments, makes a note of good deeds and also, mistakes. On the twenty-third day of the twelfth month (January in the Chinese calendar) the kitchen god travels to heaven to make his report to the Jade Emperor, the ruler of heaven. Chinese believers offer honey and incense to the kitchen god to ensure he makes a good report about them. You may enjoy making a little space for your own spiritual symbol in your kitchen. Or, light a stick of sweet–smelling incense such as vanilla or clove on a regular basis to keep the ambience in your kitchen sweet and inviting.

Dining Rooms

There are not too many rules for a dining room. Frankly, there are not too many of us who use our dining rooms for the purpose for which they were intended. If you don't want to dine in that room and you have another use for the room—such as a home business or a study area for your children—then by all means convert your dining room to that purpose. After all, it is your home and it needs to work for you.

If you need to combine purposes, for instance your dining room serves as your home office during part of the day, use baskets or other organizing containers to hide the office function when dining. Try to separate the purposes of the room so that one does not spill into the other. The goal should be that when the room is to serve as a dining room, there is not a hint of home office; and when it acts as an office, it really looks like an office and not a makeshift work area.

Example: In one well–decorated but small apartment, there was a need for the home office/dining room combination. Our solution was to find a large cabinet that could be opened to reveal a desk, computer, printer and supplies to serve as the home office center. We also found an expandable dining room table with two benches and two chairs for seating. During the day the table and benches were placed against one wall, and the desk would be opened up; in the evening, the desk would be closed, appearing to be just a beautiful piece of furniture. The table would be opened to full length easily seating six. This gave balance to this dual purpose room.

Here are a few guidelines for creating general comfort in a dining room:

There should always be an even number of chairs (it is said that otherwise one of the family members will not marry or have a stable relationship). There is no limit to the number of chairs, as long as they can be counted in pairs. However, a table that seats eight is considered very lucky. Mixing chairs at the table is fine, but all seats should be at the same height—unless you want the person at the head of the table to sit taller than the rest (a "royal" position).

The dining table should be 11–13 inches higher than the seat of the chair. Before purchasing the table, check to make sure that the tallest member of the family can cross his or her legs while seated at the table.

Round tables represent heaven and a connection with the ancestors and are thus considered to be lucky. Round tables bring happy conversation and a sense of equality to all who sit around them.

Square or other rectangular tables represent earth with its bounty and blessings, thus are also considered to be lucky. Rectangular tables have two "seats of honor," one at the head and one at the foot of the table. The person who wants power should sit at either position.

An octagonal table represents the eight main directions on a compass and thus the eight life areas of Feng Shui: Career, Benefactors, Wisdom, Family, Children, Relationships, Wealth and Reputation. This shape of table is considered to be the luckiest of all.

Ovals, hexagons and other shapes (except triangles) are considered to be neutral. Triangular tables are considered to be unlucky, as they have very sharp points, and usually only an odd number of people can sit comfortably at them.

Wooden tables represent growth both on a material and spiritual level for the entire family. (For information on the specific energy of various woods, see Chapter 11, Living Cures.) Glass tables represent good communication and the flow of feelings in the family. Stone or tile tables represent stability and help to ground the family. Grounding basically means that the family members maintain a practical and down–to–earth approach to their lives. Iron as a part of a table (I have never seen a table made completely of iron) adds a protective energy to the family as a whole.

Family Rooms

Ideally, the family room is a gathering place for everyone who resides in the home, a place where they feel both comfortable and welcome. If this is not the feeling created by your family room, it's time to take some action. Pick up this book and go sit in your family room. Visualize an ideal "family–room day" and ask yourself, "On an ideal day—be it a week or a weekend day, who else would be in the room with me?" "What would each of us be doing?"

Let us imagine together. Say that during the ideal time, perhaps an afternoon, you want to spend your time knitting. Your two children and your husband are going to watch a movie together and all four of you are going to enjoy some snacks. With this vision in mind, you know that your family room will need to offer you a comfortable chair to sit in with a nearby basket for your knitting. A seating arrangement needs to provide a clear view of the television, and offer comfortable seating for the time it takes to watch a movie. There needs to be at least one small table on which to place the snacks so that all can reach them easily. Now designing the room around this scenario is simple.

Let us try imagining another ideal "family–room day." Let's say that you want to make dinner while keeping an eye on your three children in the family room. All three have homework to do, and you have promised that the one that finishes first will be allowed to play video games for 30 minutes. So, each child needs a table to work at or a lap desk (a writing surface attached to a pillow that can be put in their lap). In addition, there would be a TV, video game console and a set of headphones so that the child playing video games would not disturb the other two still completing their homework assignments. The function would then determine your decorating plan.

Of course, the combinations are endless—this way of imagining the perfect "family room day" is an ideal way to identify the right interior design and the right Feng Shui for you (and your family). First design the day, then alter the design of the room to fit your needs. Then follow the rules for furniture placement outlined in Living Rooms, pp. 63.

While we are focusing on the family room, let's examine the subject of clutter. You have probably heard that having clutter is not good Feng Shui. Clutter disrupts the flow of Qi, it is hard on the eyes, and creates stress wherever it exists. Remember the "river of gold" we talked about in Chapter 4. Think of that gentle, meandering river now forced to flow over rocks, becoming choppy and agitated. That is what happens with the flow of Qi when it encounters clutter. As the clutter expands, it is as if the rocks in the river bed have accumulated creating a dam; all movement of the *Qi* is blocked.

Clutter is created by having stuff that has no "home," no place where it belongs, no place where it can go. In truth, it is really hard to find time to organize but the clutter is not just unpleasant to look at, to walk around, to constantly ignore—clutter is blocking your (and your family's) prosperity, your relationships, the promotion you want at work, recognition for all of the good deeds you do and your road to better health. If the *Qi* in your home is not balanced and flowing or, if it is blocked completely, then everything in your life will require more effort and more of your own energy as you attempt to manifest success. Please, clear the clutter.

Master Bedroom Bed Placement

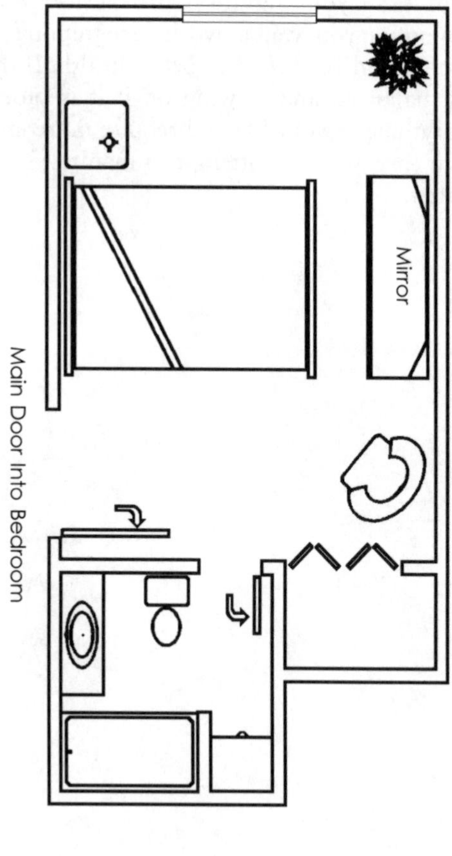

Main Door Into Bedroom

Fig. 16: This bedroom has two problems: the bed is too close to the door and across from a mirror. Sleeping in this position can cause restless sleep and health problems. A plant should be placed between the bed and the door to help protect the sleeper. A prismatic crystal should be hung in front of the mirror to break up the negative energy that comes from sleeping across from it.

Chapter 6

Feng Shui and
Your Home's Intimate Spaces

The Master Bedroom

"My relationship is dead!" the woman told me as she ushered me into her home. With one look at her bedroom I saw why. A giant cow skull was hanging over the bed. The Feng Shui question I ask myself is the same old "chicken and egg" question: Which came first? The feeling of death in the relationship—so we hang the large cow skull over the bed to symbolize that death—or, did we hang the skull up and subsequently "kill" the relationship? Sometimes I think that both things arrive simultaneously. The skull on the wall simply gives us a visible picture of what is going on beneath, in the bed.

Your bedroom is the second most important room in the house, after the kitchen. A bedroom is our sanctuary for rest, relaxation from the stresses of our lives, the place where we recuperate and where we spend time with our most intimate others. Keeping this in mind, let us take a look at your bedroom.

When I consult on a house, one of the things I am looking for is how the bedroom is decorated in relation to the rest of the house. For each person, the bedroom is their private area. How you maintain your personal and private space indicates how you treat yourself as relative to how you treat the rest of the world. If I see beautiful, elegant furnishings in the living room, dining room and family room, but find a master bedroom filled with second–hand furniture found at a yard sale, battered and uncared for, I comment on it, "It would appear that you are taking care of everyone but yourself. My advice is to take as good care of yourself as you would take of others. This will help you be around for a long time to share your life with those you care about."

Of prime importance is the placement of the bed in any bedroom, especially in the master bedroom (see figs. 16 and 17). In some systems of Feng Shui, the Feng Shui expert works with

Master Bedroom:
More Bed Placement

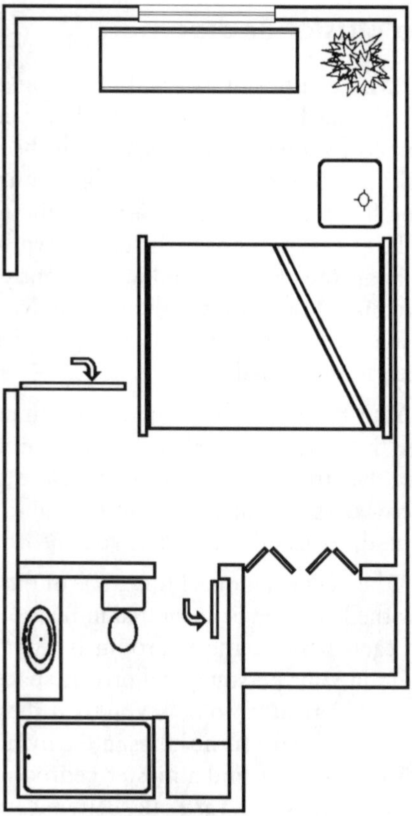

Main Door Into Bedroom

Fig. 17: This bedroom has two problems, the feet of the sleeper point out the door and one can see the commode from the bed. Sleeping in this position can cause health, sleep and career problems. Solutions include placing a mirror above the bathroom door facing into the bathroom and hanging a prismatic crystal over the bedroom door just inside the bedroom.

compass directions, determining which direction is lucky or unlucky for the individual(s) who sleep in this room. But, before you can consider the directions, it is necessary to inspect the layout of the room. Here are the rules for bed placement.

Rule #1: One should not sleep with one's feet pointing out the door. There is an old saying that when a person dies, they are carried out feet first; so, sleeping with your feet pointing out the door is considered bad for your health. The door referred to here is the main door, not a bathroom door or a patio door.

Cure: Move the bed to a new position. Or, if it is not possible to move the bed, then hang a prismatic crystal over the door into the bedroom. The crystal should be visible from the bed. This will disburse the negative Qi and keep your feet (and the rest of you) in your bed until you want to get up.

Rule #2: One should not sleep with one's feet pointing at a mirror. Some believe that the soul travels at night while we are sleeping. But if the soul, while leaving the body, should see it's reflection in a mirror, it may become frightened and leave for good. A mirror behind the bed, above the bed or beside the bed is considered acceptable—it is only when the feet of the sleeper point toward a mirror that it is considered unlucky.

Cure: The best cure is to move either the bed or the mirror. If it is not possible to move the bed or the mirror, a prismatic crystal can be used. If the mirror is part of a dresser, then crystal bottles (like perfume bottles) can sit on the dresser in front of the mirror. The crystal helps break up the Qi reflected by the mirror. Hang the crystal from a string and attach the string to the back of the dresser, allowing the crystal to drape over in front of the mirror. If the mirror is part of mirrored closet doors, it is sufficient to hang a single prismatic crystal in front of the doors. The crystal should be hung so it does not impede the opening of the doors. Again, this will help balance the flow of Qi and stop negative Qi.

Rule #3: From a reclining position, one should not be able to see a toilet. In general, the energy of the commode is considered unlucky but if one can see it while lying in bed it has an even stronger negative effect. It is believed to cause stomach and intestinal problems.

Cure: The best cure is to move the bed. If moving the bed is not an option, then keep the bathroom door closed—or at least keep the door closed enough to prevent a view of the commode. If an individual who sleeps in the room has a history of stomach or intestinal problems, it may be necessary to hang a small mirror (four inches in diameter or less) above the bathroom door facing into the bathroom. This mirror can be a simple, round mirror, or part of some decorative arrangement. This will help to keep the negative bathroom energy contained.

Rule #4: One should not sleep too close to the main bedroom door. If the room is small, the bed must sometimes be positioned very close to the door. If it is closer than three feet, it is considered to be too close for comfortable sleep. The person who sleeps on the side of the bed nearest the door (if they share the bed with another) will feel responsible for the health and safety of both of the people who share the bed, and may not sleep well, feeling the need to be watchful and on guard even while asleep.

Cure: If the bed cannot be repositioned, it is best to place a table or nightstand between the sleeper and the door. A large plant, preferably with pointed leaves, should be placed on the nightstand. This will help the sleeper feel more safe while they slumber.

Rule #5: A bed should be placed on a solid wall. This is important if the person who sleeps in the bed has a history of sinus problems or if the sleeper is a child. Placing the bed on a solid wall gives the sleeper the feeling of support. Children who sleep next to a window may feel that they are vulnerable to a stranger looking in, even if their room is on an upper floor. If there is a history of sinus problems, then the draft from windows will not help the sleeper.

Cure: If the bed cannot be placed on a solid wall, place a mirror in the window, facing out. The mirror can be small (less than one inch in diameter) and can be taped to the glass.

Rule #6: The bed of an adult should not be on more than one wall. If the bed is placed in the corner so that both the head and one side are on walls it provides too much support, acting like a crutch, holding back the individual from independent action. If two people sleep in a bed that is on two walls, the person who sleeps next to the wall will feel no sense of independence, and will have their life dictated by the will of others.

Cure: Leave at least enough room for the occupant(s) of the bed to exit from either side.

Rule #7: One should not sleep under something heavy. Large paintings or posters framed with glass should not be placed above the bed because if they fall down, they will injure the sleeper.

Rule #8: Likewise, it is considered unlucky to have ceiling fans directly over the sleeper's chest or head, because even though the fans are secured to the ceiling, the motion and the weight they represent can disrupt a person's sleep. It is believed that if the fan is positioned above a sleeper's head, the individual will have sinus problems; if the fan is positioned over the sleeper's heart, the individual will have chest trouble; and if the fan is positioned over the stomach, the sleeper will have stomach and intestinal problems.

Rule #9: One should not sleep next to heavy furniture. Very tall, very heavy pieces should not be placed next to a bed. The rule is: the height of the furniture is the minimum distance to the bed. A heavy dresser, for example, is too close if it would hit the sleeper should it fall over. The "pressure" from large objects next to the bed can cause a disruption of regular sleep patterns.

Rule #10: Neutralize any poison arrows. Poison arrows are common in bedrooms—especially if the bedroom has a built-in closet or private bathroom. A poison arrow is created when a corner protrudes into the room (see diagram). Poison arrows are a serious problem if the arrow (or corner) points to the bed. This can divide the Qi, causing problems between a couple who share the bed, or can create personal stress for an individual.

Cure: Poison arrows can be cured in several ways. Bell strings or hanging plants can be hung in front of the protruding corner, or one can place a piece of furniture between the bed and the arrow. This neutralizes the sha Qi of the poison arrow.

Feng Shui to Improve Your Personal Life

If you are seeking change in your personal and intimate relationships, if you are not sleeping well, if you are ill or recovering from an illness too slowly, you may want to alter the Qi in your bedroom overall. Here are a few specific suggestions.

To attract a relationship first stop repelling them. Examine the décor of your bedroom and ask yourself if you would feel comfortable inviting a lover into the room. Are you proud of how the room looks? Or, is it in such disarray that both you and your prospective partner would have to climb over the clutter just to get to the bed? Create a welcoming environment for yourself and for the potential "someone" you might like to invite into your private space.

Remove teddy bears, stuffed animals and other toys that are reminders of childhood. These types of toys are given to children who have to sleep alone. They may be providing you with comfort but keeping you from attracting the comfort you need from a living, breathing other.

Remove pictures of Mom and Dad, Grandma and other family members. Pictures of family should be placed in family rooms, living rooms, hallways, etc. Your bedroom is your private place. (Remember, it is hard to be passionate with an intimate other in front of Mom and Dad.) Also, and for a similar reason, keep religious items to a minimum. Unless sexuality is a major part of your religious expression, keep only a few spiritual icons in the bedroom. These are better placed in the living room, kitchen, family room or dining room.

Remove any décor that is a reminder of the past or of death and sadness. Remove dried flower arrangements, pictures of cold, icy landscapes and skeletons or skulls of dead animals (no cow skulls with horns, no matter how attractively they may have been preserved or decorated). If you are in a happy relationship, limit your selection of these types of items to one per room. More than that will give you an attachment to the past while healthy and happy relationships are based on current loving and supportive experiences, mutual growth and a vision of the future.

To attract a new relationship, buy new sheets. I have known some clients to get an entire new bed. They felt that their old bed held the Qi of the old relationship (or lack thereof) and that a new bed would bring new relationships and love into their lives. If you cannot afford a new bed, buy the sheets—preferably in a different color than ones you have had before. (See Chapter 15, Colors, pp. 206) will provide for lots of ideas about the different kinds of Qi each color attracts. (However, let me give you a little hint here: try red!)

Treat yourself to some new pajamas or a pretty nightgown. The purpose of these exercises is to prepare yourself mentally and emotionally to welcome a guest into your bedroom. Hang a single bell or a string of bells near the bed. Bells call new *Qi* into a space (see pp. 163, Bells, for more information). Chime them often. The sound tells the Universe that you are open to love and are calling in a new relationship.

To rid yourself of an old, no longer desired relationship, start by removing that *Qi* from your personal space. Remove any of their clothing, books, pictures and knick–knacks from the room. If the objects are ones you want to keep, clear them by using salt or sage. If the individual still has not moved out of your home, place salt crystals under their shoes and in a dish under their side of the bed. Salt removes attachments to people (and things), and will cause them to feel unattached to you and to the house. This lack of attachment will be an encouragement to them to find somewhere else to be. Once they move out, give yourself new sheets and new pillow cases (or new pillows) and start fresh.

Sometimes people have trouble sleeping. If that is happening to you, remove anything that is under your bed. Clean and keep the area under your bed perfectly clear of any storage or clutter for the time being. Next, choose restful colors for your décor. Consider pinks, pastels or tans. It would be best to paint the walls but if that is not possible, at least change out the bedspread and the sheets. Also, consider wearing night clothes in pastel colors (not white).

Some herbs promote sleep. Place chamomile or lavender—either a plant or some dried herb—next to the bed. Consider adding other plants to the environment, too. Plants give off oxygen and can help you relax. Remove any paper, bills and calendars from your immediate sleeping area. It is best not to store files in the bedroom. Keep the room very dark; add black–out curtains to the windows if necessary. Place "sleepy" art in the room, pictures of a sleepy town, sleeping cats, restful scenes and quiet interiors.

Also, too many electronics can disturb sleep, even if you are not using them. Remove excess electronics such as the television, computer and stereo, etc., from the bedroom. Watching too much television is like getting a restless sleep. It gives your body and mind nothing it really needs. So if you really have trouble sleeping, give up the television for a few days and try reading; see if your sleep improves.

When you are recovering from an illness, it is best to decorate the room with colors that promote health and healing and ones that keep you grounded (that is, conscious of your body and your surroundings in the present moment). Avoid pinks and purples in the bedroom at such times, and choose greens, browns, tans and other earth tones. If you cannot change your wall color, at least change the bedspread and sheets. Plants promote wellness. If the room is too dark for live plants, consider silk ones. Plants are symbols of good health.

Decorate the walls with lively pictures of children playing, happy people and wonderful places you want to visit. Choose rich landscapes, travel posters and maps. Place your remedies and treatments or medicines in a convenient drawer out of sight unless it is time to take them. Only leave medical equipment in clear sight if you must use it constantly. Clear the air and *Qi* every few days using incense, essential oils or by opening the window for a good airing (weather permitting). Use a fan occasionally to help the *Qi* and the air circulate.

Miscellaneous Tips

1. If you want to move and are unable to find the means or the energy to do so, move your bed away from all walls in the bedroom. Allowing the bed to "float" in the room energetically removes the support you have been receiving from your current residence and allows (or requires) you to become more independent of your immediate circumstances. You will no longer feel attached to the house and therefore it will become easier for you to move.

2. If you would like to become pregnant (or to have children), it is considered unwise to clean under the bed. Feng Shui lore dictates that the soul of the baby visits his or her mother–to–be and that if you clean under your bed you may frighten the baby away. Likewise, no furniture should be moved in the bedroom of a woman who is pregnant—this again so as not to frighten away the soul of the baby.

3. An individual's bedroom should not be visible from the front door. When your bed can be seen by visitors they can come to

feel "intimate" with you much too quickly and may therefore take liberties they would otherwise not have dared to take. You may find that people ask for favors and expect special treatment from you very soon after you have met them. In matters of the heart, you will attract relationships that become physically intimate quickly (which may or may not be a good thing).

4. Feng Shui lore tells of an ancient cure for backaches: place a piece of chalk under the exact spot where the afflicted person sleeps. This is said to alleviate the back pain. (Well, it certainly couldn't hurt!)

5. Just one more thought...the master bedroom is for the master(s) of the house. Whoever sleeps in that bedroom will control the household—even if that individual is a child. There are no exceptions to this rule. You may think that because of the size or the location of the room within the house that it is more suitable for the twins or your visiting mother–in–law, but heed this warning: the person who sleeps/resides in the master bedroom rules the house.

Bedroom / Home Office

Sometimes a bedroom has to serve multiple purposes. If your bedroom is also your home office, you must take special care to separate the two areas of the room. Create a "zone" for the home office and another for the bedroom area. Then do not let objects (e.g., paper, blankets, books and pillows) cross the line. Use a screen to separate the bed from the desk, the electronics, etc. Better still, use a cabinet for your desk then close it up when it is bed time.

Bedroom / Exercise Room

Many people now use their bedroom as their exercise and fitness room. If this is the case in your home, try separating the bed from the fitness equipment using a folding screen or a curtain. Also, exercise equipment does not impart good health Qi if used as a clothing rack. If you begin to use it as a clothes hanger, you are not going to use it for exercise. In that case, move your fitness equipment to the garage where it will no longer take up space and Qi in your bedroom.

Children's Room: Bed Placement

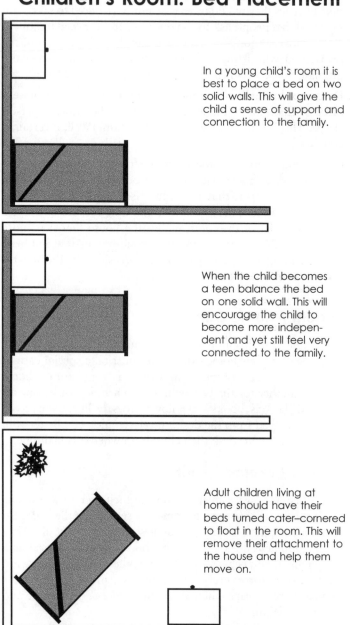

In a young child's room it is best to place a bed on two solid walls. This will give the child a sense of support and connection to the family.

When the child becomes a teen balance the bed on one solid wall. This will encourage the child to become more independent and yet still feel very connected to the family.

Adult children living at home should have their beds turned cater-cornered to float in the room. This will remove their attachment to the house and help them move on.

Children's Bedroom(s)

When considering good Feng Shui treatments for a child's room, first consider the age of the child. Small children are dependent on you for protection, food, clothing and shelter. Then there are grown children who are either not ready to "leave the nest" or who are unable to leave for a variety of reasons. The use of Feng Shui techniques differs for these situations.

When children are young it is important that they feel safe in their room(s). If they do not, they may end up sleeping with you more than is beneficial for them or you. Without the sense of safety in their own room(s) they may become fearful and dependent on others. And while being dependent on one's parents may be fine, it can cause a child to become a follower of anyone who claims to provide a sense of safety.

That being noted, it is important to listen to what the child is afraid of in their bedroom—whether it be under the bed, in the closet or perhaps a particular toy that makes strange shadows. Arming a child with their own flashlight can help a lot. But it sometimes helps if the child can choose a "protector." Some children might choose a religious figure, statue or painting. Sometimes they identify an animal figure (perhaps a lion or bear), sometimes it is a picture of a relative. Place this protector near the bed, pointing at the door. This can help calm the child's fears.

Additionally, it is important to set the bed in a supportive place in the room. If your child needs a lot of support, place the bed in a corner on two walls (one at the head and one on a side of the bed). Walls provide a sense of security for children. For this reason a child's bed should not "float" in the room or be placed cater-cornered. A bed that floats out into the room causes the sleeper to need to be completely independent. Small children usually cannot handle this feeling of complete autonomy and they will seek to sleep with you.

Teenagers, on the other hand, start to feel less connected to their family, and need less support from their parents and siblings. They will prefer a sense of independence and spend less and less time at home. As a child grows into their teens, ideally, the bed can be moved so only the head of the bed is on a solid wall. This will allow them to feel more free, yet still connected to the family.

When the "child" reaches his or her late teens and early adulthood, encourage them to place their bed at an angle in the room. This will remove their attachment to the "apron strings" and help them to develop a strong sense of self for their future on their own. I have often seen grown children who have returned the position of their bed to the one best in early childhood—pushing it up against two walls in their bedroom at home. They are unconsciously anchoring themselves to the house and are actively attracting more support from other family members.

Other rules for bed placement in a child's room are the same as those for an adult's bedroom. The sleeper should not have his or her head too close to a door. One should not sleep: in view of a toilet, with one's feet pointing out a door, under heavy objects, or across from a mirror.

Example: When I was young (preteen), string art was all the rage. One took a board, pounded in at least a hundred six–penny nails. Then the artist (myself, in this case) wrapped colored string around the nails making pretty geometric patterns. A fine example of string art was hung over my bed, it probably measured two feet on a side and weighed at least thirty pounds. One night I will never forget, I sat up in bed quite suddenly, a moment later the wooden board fell on my pillow behind me. This provides a dramatic Feng Shui lesson: all heavy objects should be kept away from the sleeper—especially if the sleeper is a child. Keep the head of the bed clear of shelves, heavy pictures or pictures with glass and the child will sleep better.

Clutter in Children's Rooms

Most Feng Shui practitioners will tell you that clutter is bad— no matter where it is or what it consists of. However, it is important to understand the reasons behind the creation of clutter. These vary based on the situation. For instance, in the case of a child's room, the definition of clutter must be adjusted according to their age. Very young children have a short attention span. They are learning things at a remarkable rate; they are experimenting constantly and this process creates a lot of clutter. An item is pulled out of a storage box but then something else catches their eye and the first object is forgotten. Then there is a call to dinner and all is forgotten again.

Clutter in a child's room mirrors the frenetic energy going on in their active imaginations. Now, some young children will be very neat—a reflection of their thinking process, which is more orderly and calm. Others will create a great mess and as long as it is contained in their room (not causing every inch of the family's living space in the house to be overwhelmingly cluttered), there is no harm in it.

As children grow older they no longer need the great stimuli of so many colors and shapes scattered on the floor to trigger their imagination and the growth of their minds. Clutter now is the result of an entirely different reason, clutter is used for protection. Teenagers have little control in their lives. They usually have limited financial resources, no car and little say in where they go; also, they may not be free to choose who they can (and cannot) see. So, the one thing they can control in all of their world is the floor of their bedroom. Clutter is the one thing they can do to protect their space. If their room is chaotic and clutter is everywhere—it is camouflage. We may not even know they are in the room and so, in a sense, they feel safe. As long as the clutter remains only in their room, it is fine.

The clutter problem here is that if you clean up their room (or have them do it), you remove the safety it represents. With no safety, they are likely to lash out in anger, to be sad or just scared. The child's room is only going to get messy again. So, don't fight it. Give them a territory—their own room—and allow them to make it as messy as they want. Agree with them that you will honor their space as long as they keep all of their mess contained in that one room.

Previously I have mentioned that Qi moves very roughly over clutter. Clutter disrupts the flow of the Qi, and having a lot of choppy Qi in your home makes it difficult to balance the overall energy of the home. It is possible to have so much clutter that the flow of the Qi is completely stopped. But if the clutter is being used for protection and you remove that protection, you may find less balance of energy than you ever had before. One messy room will not disrupt the flow of the Qi in the entire house, especially if it occurs in a room with a door that can be shut.

When dealing with teenage children, allow them some clutter. Remember the last time you felt completely powerless in your world—maybe due to a difficult job situation, a challenging relationship issue or your own parents when you were younger. This will allow you to feel a bit of what it is like to be a teenager again. Allow your teen to create a "world" in their room, one that feels safe to them. One day you may find that the clutter has disappeared and this will be because they have found a sense of safety on their own, and are discovering their own ability to handle their world on their terms.

When your children have come of age and it's time for them to leave the family home, then it is time for the clutter to be gone. No adult child should have a cluttered room. When it is time to move out, these adults—who stay in your home either with your permission or without it—need to have completely clutter–free rooms. If an adult child is living in clutter, they are doing this so that you do not find them and remove them from their all too comfortable and responsibility–free life. Here the clutter has a more detrimental effect on the household as a whole, as it can block opportunities for new jobs, new relationships and new living arrangements.

Guest Bedrooms

Guest bedrooms are treated entirely differently than the rest of the house from the perspective of Feng Shui. The rules that are so important in other rooms change when we enter a guest bedroom. The placement of furniture in the guest room is influenced greatly by how much you want to have guests and how long you want them to stay. Sometimes a person has a guest room because they feel obligated to have one; others welcome guests and want them to stay as long as they like. The auspicious furniture placement discussed under the topic "The Master Bedroom" above would only apply if you want your guests to feel very much at home and stay as long as possible. Otherwise, furniture can be placed so your guests feel comfortable while they stay with you, but they won't overstay their welcome.

The key to decorating a guest room for the temporary guest is to place the furniture just slightly "off." Notice the next hotel room you stay in while on vacation or in Las Vegas, for instance. In Las Vegas the hotel wants you to visit but not to stay in your room. So the rooms are comfortable but slightly off energetically to push you out of the room and back into the casinos and activities going on around town. (This is not true for some of the finer rooms but since these are generally provided for "high rollers" it is not necessary to entice them out of their rooms.) Notice in a hotel room how often poison arrows point into the room. The protruding corner will either point to the bed or will block the view to the door.

In the case of a guest bedroom in your home, you need to decide how many guests you want and for how long. If you are using the room for a dual purpose (such as a home office/guest room or an exercise/guest room you may welcome guests but it may be difficult to accommodate them for long without their visit interrupting your daily life. In this case, rooms should be designed for the comfort of your family rather than the guest because you and your family members will be the primary users of the space.

When I see guest rooms that are much more attractively and expensively decorated than other bedrooms in the home I know that one or both of the principle owners of the house is more interested in pleasing outsiders than in taking care of themselves. Such an interest in the well–being of others can be considered a virtue but in this case creates a energy imbalance. From a Feng Shui perspective, your house is your home and not a hotel. So, most of the focus needs to be centered first on the master bedroom, next on the children's room(s), then accommodation for pets and only then on the guest rooms. This actually shows your guests no disrespect, instead it demonstrates loyalty to those in your home who love and support you every day. (If you live with people who do not love and support you, that is an entirely different issue.)

Now, if you are setting up a bedroom for a person who will come and stay for a long time—months or years—then follow the rules laid down for a child's bedroom. Do not set them up in the master bedroom unless you want them to be master of the house. It is better to give them autonomy in their own quarters, not over the entire household.

If you are setting up a guest bedroom for someone convalescing from a serious illness or surgery, pay particular attention to color and décor. Choose design items and colors that encourage healing and grounding. (Note: Grounding in this context means that the individual who will sleep in the room is conscious of their body and its own healing powers, they are aware of their physical feelings and sensations but not experiencing pain. When grounded, an individual is more apt to participate in their own healing process and thus heal much more quickly. We just want to create the most positive flow of *Qi* in the environment that we possible can to enhance and support the healing process.)

When a Feng Shui expert considers an appropriate color for a bedroom, we look at the walls, floor coverings and bedding. In a room of this nature we might consider shades of green, blue and peach—either separately or together. Green is the color of growth, health and wellness and can help speed healing. Blue gives a sense of peace and mental balance which leads to understanding communications with others in the household and easy sleep for the guest. Peach is a soft, warm color that aids sleep while simultaneously giving energy for healing. Smaller knick–knacks and decorative objects in the room can be of any color. However, avoid shades of pink because it is a color associated with physical weakness and it can mask or inhibit communication about problems. Also avoid shades of purple because it is a color that is connected to the spiritual experience not the physical body and it does not enhance a person's ability to remain grounded while healing.

There are specific symbols we can add into the décor of the room when the individual residing in it is recovering from illness. Peach, the fruit, is a symbol of long life, as is bamboo. Pictures of plants (especially peaches or bamboo) and growing things bring a vital, living and healthy energetic quality to the *Qi* in the room. Articles made of jade—even small pieces—promote longevity. Tortoise shell, the shell of a creature that lives a very long life, is used to create items that may be perfect decorations for this room. Little statues, pictures or images woven into fabrics are all helpful. Of course, avoid symbols that speak of death: skulls, desert scenes, graveyards and sunsets. Too much black or too much white should also be avoided (white is the color of mourning in the Chinese culture).

Example: A wonderful A–frame house in a lush, forest–like setting was so frequented by guests that friends of the owners were "booking" time to visit. One look at the guest room and I knew why. It was a large room on the second floor with a high ceiling and bay windows overlooking a meadow of flowers. The bed was perfectly placed, the décor tasteful and peaceful. I felt as if I wanted to stay there myself. The solution to their guest problem was to move their home office up to the beautiful room, giving their business as much consideration as they had been giving their guests. I also suggested moving their current guest and the guest room furniture to a smaller, less inviting room.

If you want your guests to feel welcome and comfortable, but you don't want them to overstay their welcome, decorate with bright colors—especially primary colors: red, blue and yellow—used in combination. Choose a décor that has a more temporary feel: fresh cut flowers, pictures of butterflies, ocean waves (they move in and out with the tides) and hummingbirds. Avoid placing heavy objects in the room. These can weigh down the *Qi* moving through the room; especially avoid furniture or decorative touches of marble, granite or clay. If there is a clay tile floor in the room, consider placing a rug over it. Place any growing plants in wooden containers rather than clay ones.

If you are providing a guest room purely from a sense of social obligation (you don't really want guests to come or stay in your home at all), choosing the right décor can help you reach your objective. To entirely frighten guests away, plan a décor of a slightly "scary" nature. Items placed attractively around your guest room might include gargoyles, stark black and white photos, dried flowers, pictures of winter scenes and so on. These colors encourage people to spend a minimum of time. Or you can choose, instead of a bed, a piece of furniture that disguises its purpose. A futon or sofa bed is an ideal choice (especially if it must be made up each morning and night). This allows you plenty of opportunities to hide the fact that you have a guest room at all.

Example: One very patient mother, plagued by the constant returning of her college–graduate daughter, finally placed a very large (and quite scary) doll in the guest room of her home. Immediately after returning home to stay for a while, her daughter asked that the doll be removed. But the mother said that it had to stay in the room, because there was no where else to put it. The daughter soon found both a new job and an apartment of her own, and my client was able to enjoy some peace and quiet at home—and continue a pleasant, loving relationship with her daughter.

As you can see, the rules for placing furniture in a guest room are quite different from those suggested for the other bedrooms. If you want to demonstrate the power of Feng Shui for yourself, try different arrangements with different guests and observe their reaction. It can be a most interesting and informative exercise.

Bathrooms

Bathrooms are the most maligned rooms in current Feng Shui literature. A great many cures are suggested and many have been tried and tested down through the years. Let's set the record straight. Despite that some books say the bathroom is a source of negative energy, let me tell you that it is good to have a bathroom or bathrooms in your home. None of us would be happy if we did not have them, so it is not OK from a Feng Shui perspective to treat a bathroom as if it were some dreadful room designed to drain away all of the money and Qi from your home. Contrary to what you may have read, your drains do not need to be plugged all the time. And if you have placed a mirror above your toilet, you can take it down. These are mistranslations of the traditional texts, and are really not necessary.

Yes, some money Qi does leave your house every day. Thank goodness it does! Otherwise the mortgage or the rent would not be paid, food would not be purchased, and you would have a very sparse wardrobe. Our main goal with Feng Shui is to attract an abundance of good Qi, that flows through the house. For there to be flow, some (or at least a little) Qi must go through our space and out into the universe again. As long as we can attract more Qi into our lives than flows out of it, we will be fine. With this in mind, here are a few rules for bathrooms.

Rule #1: Keep the toilet lid down. Feng Shui's gift to woman–kind was providing a reason for the males in her life to put the seat (or the lid) down. It is not fun for anyone, male or female, to walk into a bathroom and immediately be looking into the toilet bowl. And anything that is unattractive, disturbs the energy and is not good Feng Shui. Keeping the lid down helps every member of the household to both retain their money and their good health.

Rule #2: Drains can be open/uncovered. While we don't want to be looking into the toilet, it is not as distracting to have open drains. In truth, whatever is going down these drains is probably not something you want to keep anyway. It is very disruptive for an individual in the home to feel that they must constantly monitor the drains in every bathroom in the house. Like I said before, it is perfectly all right for some *Qi* to exit the house in a normal, controlled fashion—just as long as we are bringing in more.

Rule #3: Keep faucets in good working order. Drips are an entirely different consideration. Drips mean that your money is leaking away. Small unexpected expenses eat away at paycheck after paycheck leaving you with very little. Fix all drips immediately. Because even a small drip can add up to a large loss of money over time.

Rule #4: Keep drains clear. A stopped–up drain or toilet is bad for health. Keep the pipes in the bathroom (and the kitchen for that matter) clear. This will support your own intestinal health and the health of other family members.

Rule #5: Choose colors based on your personal needs. Avoid pastel color choices in the bathroom(s) of your home if you are recovering from illness. As in the bedroom, if you are working to improve you health, you need the energy of grounding colors selected from the green and brown palettes. You may also need the extra energy offered by bright colors like reds and blues. Stay away from pinks, lavenders and other pale colors.

One final tip, there is a saying in Feng Shui that says if a guest washes their hands in one of your bathrooms, money will come to you. So make sure you have soap and towels available for your guests.

Home Office

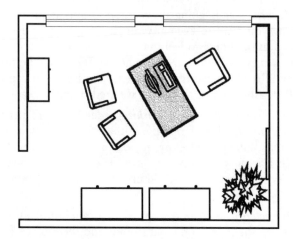

Fig. 18: If space is abundant, set the desk in the command position floating it in the room with a view of the door and a view out a window. Place guest chairs in the subordinate position with backs to the door.

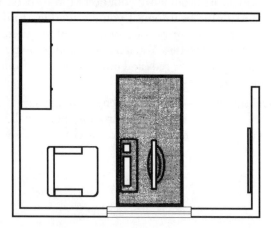

Fig. 19: In smaller offices the desk should be positioned on one wall only, also with a view of the door and out a window (if available). This gives the person a view of what is coming now (door) and in the long term future (outside).

Chapter 7

Feng Shui in Other Rooms and Other Spaces

Home Office

The rules for a home office are different than for every other room in the house. The home office is your family's special place for attracting wealth. If you don't have a separate room serving as an office in your home, at least have a space that is dedicated to balancing your check books, paying your bills and working with your investments. Without a specific space in your home for working on the family's financial and wealth goals, it will be very difficult to attract sufficient money Qi to satisfy the needs and wants everyone has. If your home office is part of your dining room or bedroom, take special care to separate the room into the specific zones so that the energy of one does not negatively affect the other. Much of Feng Shui is about attracting prosperity and money into our lives, and one of the best (and easiest) ways to attract wealth is to maintain an energetically well–balanced home office space.

The rules for placing furniture in this room/space are different from the ones mentioned previously for other rooms because the type of Qi you want to attract to this area is about power rather than harmony. We want moving Qi rather than a relaxed, quietly flowing type of Qi. You need to attract confidence rather than comfort. Here are the rules for placing furniture in your home office:

Rule #1: The desk should face the door. Let me qualify that: when you are sitting at your desk you should be able to see the door (see figs. 18 and 19). It doesn't matter whether the door is to the right or left of you or directly in front of you but it should not be to your back. It is considered highly unlucky if you work with your back to the door. This is a subordinate position and this energy can affect other areas of your life. Sitting with your back to the door is the standard "cubicle position"—a position the boss would never sit in. You are the master of your own financial destiny at home and in your life, so if at all possible, do not place your desk in a subordinate's position in your home office.

Rule #2: The desk should not touch more than one wall. In fact, it is perfectly fine from the perspective of Feng Shui if the desk "floats" in the room. Walls are for support but a desk situated against more than one wall will cause you to feel dependent on others. In time you may find great restrictions and limitations on your ability to make independent decisions and choices. It is all right to have one side of the desk against a wall, but avoid having two or three sides of the desk do so.

Rule #3: The individual working at the desk should sit with a view out a window. In addition to a view of the door, there should be a view out a window. If it is a pleasant vista, so much the better. An office with a window gives the person who sits there a perspective on life. The view outside represents a picture of the future while the view inside symbolizes the present. This allows you to change perspective from now to the future and back again. This helps with long–term planning and setting long–term goals.

Rule #4: While you do want a view out a window, there should not be a distracting glare or a sharp, unyielding light from the window. Too much light can inhibit your ability to work comfortably at your desk or computer screen. While you certainly want to have a window in your home office, you don't need to have the shades open at all times. Nor do you really want to face a window because the glare can be hard on the eyes.

Rule #5: Place nothing heavy over your desk. If there are shelves above the desk, do not fill and overload them with heavy books and notebooks. Having heavy objects above your head can cause a lot of unconscious or subconscious pressure, resulting in headaches, neck problems, worry, etc. Sitting under heavy objects and clutter can cause procrastination and make it difficult to concentrate.

Rule #6: Keep clutter to a minimum. You are probably getting tired of hearing me say this. And you are probably wondering when you are going to find time in your busy schedule to take care of all of this clutter. Most clutter in office situations suggests more of an organizational problem than a space problem. It's not that we don't want to be organized—we are just not sure how best to do it.

Here are a few tips I share with my business and corporate clients to help them organize an overloaded desk and office space:

Group like items. If you have trouble finding things when you need them, try grouping similar items all in the same place in the office (or in a home). For instance, I keep a small box marked "glue" in my home office. It contains all types of glue: glue stick, glue gun, white glue, even nail glue (it has 1,001 uses). Now, this does mean that if I am upstairs and I need glue, I must go downstairs to my office to get it—and I need to return it there after I have used it. On the other hand, I always know exactly where the glue is so I save a lot of time not having to rummage through drawers or cabinets in several rooms.

Divide big projects into smaller segments. Do not try to Feng Shui the whole house at one time, and don't try to organize your entire home office at one time. Work on one small area—say, the upper left hand corner of your desk. Give this area a name (in Feng Shui call it the "wealth area of the desk" because if we were to divide up the top of your desk using the Black Hat system of Feng Shui, this is where the wealth area would be). Start with this area, removing clutter and organizing it to create a flow of positive Qi. You may want to place a goal list here. When this area is clear and organized then you can move to other areas of the desk or even the room.

Use the "one item in/one item out" method. If you are going to keep a piece of paper, find a piece of paper you can toss. If you are going to add a knick–knack to the shelf in your office, find one you can move somewhere else or donate to a good cause.

Everything needs a place. Everything should have a home. If something doesn't have a place, assign it one today. If it doesn't work for you to have it in the new place, well, you can always reassign it to another new location tomorrow.

Place something red on the desk. The color red, placed in the lower field of vision, helps us make decisions. Place your phone on a red blotter to make you more confident and decisive when you make calls. Or, place something red under the computer to improve your written communication skills via emails, presentations and marketing.

Have a symbol of moving water in your office. This will increase and improve monetary flow. Moving water may be in the form of a fountain, a fish tank or a picture of moving water such as a waterfall, ocean waves or a bubbling stream. Hang pictures or place fountains in view of the desk. Fish tanks can be placed behind the desk and away from windows. (For more information on fountains and fish tanks, see Moving Cures, pp. 191.)

I believe that a genetic memory exists inside each of us—a memory from the time when paper was precious and the things written on paper were priceless. Now information comes to us in waves, overwhelming amounts of it from the television, internet, print media, photos and voice messages. But we still, at some deeper level, believe that all of this information is important and that we may need it for our survival. This is no longer true and we need to learn to let go.

All this being said, people have different work styles and your style may tolerate some clutter. But try to keep some free space on your desk at all times. Free space will help attract new opportunities and provide some "breathing room." Review what surrounds your desk and remove items that are not often used. Find organizing boxes or baskets to help keep extra clutter off of the desk.

Desk/Workspace

Now, regarding the desk itself: rectangular desks are not any better or worse than L–shaped ones. However, with the L–shaped desk make sure you have an easy way in and out of the desk—otherwise you may become chained to your job. Wooden desks represent growth and a desire to expand business. Desks of wood veneer covering man–made–material bring a desire to take quick action and to be efficient. Glass desks represent good communication and an ability to receive help from others. Metal–supported desks (either with a wood top or a glass top) add energy for wealth and a focus on money. Stone or tile inserts in a desk add stability to the business operation. They help to keep work flowing at a balanced and manageable pace.

When I see someone's home office, I often know a great deal about their method of doing business. I can see where their strengths are and what they need to work on. The furniture and décor symbolize the energy attracted to the business. This can show the businesses strengths and challenges. Below is a list of the most common problems I see in home offices:

1. The décor is not inviting. If you work at home you should be excited about your office—looking forward to whatever part of your day that will be spent in it. The décor of the home office should not be an afterthought.

2. No comfortable chair. You are not going to compel yourself to work harder by making yourself uncomfortable. Give yourself a good chair—especially if you have to sit for long periods of time.

3. Too many distractions. If your desk is topped with a hundred small sticky–notes, the television is on in the corner and "ping!" you just received a fresh batch of email spam—it's no wonder that you can't accomplish anything, much less finish.

4. Lots of piles with things jumbled together mean, "If I don't see it, I will forget it. And now I am working on learning to forget even the things I can see." In–boxes, out–boxes, and to–do–boxes are great for organizing but not good for storage. If you feel that you will forget something if it is not right there in plain view then you need a new system.

5. Lots of sticky–notes mean, "If I nag myself sufficiently, I will get it (or at least something) done." Decorating your monitor with a thousand sticky notes just looks cluttered. And you are only teaching yourself to ignore what is right in front of you. Place notes to yourself in a notebook and review it daily to remind yourself of current projects.

6. Prominently displayed trash means, "I am too busy to look at new opportunities." Keep the trash can out of sight.

7. Toys on the desk mean, "I would rather be doing anything else…" One or two toys represent creative expression, many toys just bring distraction.

8. Lots of business cards on the desk mean, "I have trouble delegating my time and energy." Each card represents either a person you need to make contact with, a person who you may want to someday make contact with, or a piece of paper to

toss. With these categories in mind sort quickly through the cards and reduce the pile on your desk.

9. Broken or mismatched desk accessories mean, "My work is not important enough to invest a little money in it."

One final thought: If you are working out of your home or managing a part time business that you hope will one day replace your "9 to 5," it will benefit you greatly to create an office you love to spend time working in. If you have a house filled with fine furniture and the décor of the home office consists of a card table and a hand–me–down chair, you are not valuing what you can bring into your life through that office nor are you valuing the time you spend in it. The more you depend on the income generated by your home office, the more you need to avoid making your space a "dumping ground" for hand–me–down furniture, old broken chairs and a storage area of junk.

Some of the office superstores have new lines of furniture that look great, at very reasonable prices. Give yourself a comfortable chair, a nice desk and as many things as you need to stay organized. This will help you attract beneficial, prosperous Qi to your business or part–time venture.

Specialty Rooms

The most commonly expressed wish of both house and apartment dwellers is for a room of their own. People these days crave a room where they can spread out and think, a room where they can be quiet or where they can be loud, a room where they can be creative or receptive, energetic or lazy. Most of all they wish for a space to call their own.

It is not necessary to devote an entire room to create a space for yourself. Sometimes just a corner of a room, decorated to attract positive Qi and to provide that feeling of personal expression and comfort will be enough. However, if you have an extra room in your home, then by all means make that room your sanctuary.

Because specialty rooms are rooms devoted to a single purpose, there are special rules governing each type of space.

Craft Rooms

If you are lucky enough to have room or space in your home which can be devoted entirely to crafts, here are a few things to keep in mind:

Rule #1: Keep clutter to a minimum. Keep floors clear of pins, needles and other sharp objects. While some clutter can spark creativity and objects jumbled together can bring inspiration, you want to leave some clear space for new creative energy to come in and it's nice to have a little room to work on your projects.

Rule #2: Don't have more than a couple of unfinished projects visible at any one time. To really heighten the completion *Qi*, have only one unfinished project on the table at a time. Store unfinished projects in labeled bins under a table or in a closet. These can then be pulled out whenever you feel inspired to work on them.

To attract more creative *Qi* into this space, decorate with bright colors. Paint the walls with oranges, blues, reds and yellows or other bright, flashy colors. Decorate with brightly colored storage boxes and colorful throw rugs. Make the room fun. If you get stuck creatively, clear the room energetically using bells, salt or smudge (See Clearing a Space, pp. 133, for more information.)

Game Rooms

If you house is large enough, you may have a game room. A game room is usually defined as the room with the billiard table. But these days, game rooms can also be devoted to video games, pinball machines, air hockey and so on. A game room serves as a great addition to the house because often it helps keep the clutter and noise contained to one area. Here are a few guidelines:

Rule #1: Make sure the room is large enough for the activities you have planned. Even though clutter will find its way here, try to keep it to a minimum. Consider shelves or bins for half–finished creative projects and labeled boxes for games and video game equipment. Paint the room bright colors or dark colors (for television viewing). This creates *Qi* that helps make time for fun in your life.

Rule #2: If the room is small then keep only toys that are used often. As children become too old for toys or become tired of their games, get together with them and help them choose which ones they will donate to charity. Have them donate old toys (or old games) before new toys arrive (for birthdays and holidays). This will give them good habits for a non–cluttered future.

Exercise Rooms

With so much interest in health and physical fitness these days, many of us are creating a special place for our exercise equipment (some of which is huge) and space where we can do our workout routines. As you organize your exercise room, here are a few special Feng Shui considerations. They are important because this room will be used very intensely for short periods (usually less than a couple of hours each day) and any individual using the equipment or the space will usually be in constant motion while in the room.

Rule #1: The room should be attractive. The most important factor in creating an exercise room is to make it sufficiently attractive and welcoming to encourage you to spend time in it. Paint the walls a color you really like. Decorate in earth tones, colors which are more grounding, rather than purples, lavenders or pinks which are not as physically empowering. Hang pictures of wonderful nature scenes of places you would like to visit or where you might want to spend time: beaches, mountains, big cities—whatever inspires you.

Rule #2: Design an efficient room where you can complete your workout comfortably. Give yourself enough space to move about so you will not be hitting walls or the ceiling as you carry out your program. Set up the equipment so you don't have to spend a lot of time moving pieces from one place to another. Add a clock and a calendar to mark your progress.

Rule #3: Create a healthful environment so that the Qi circulating in the room contributes to your personal health. Make sure there is good ventilation. Consider using paint and carpet that are eco–friendly. Add living plants to the décor to promote health—or, if there is no space for living plants, add pictures of plants.

Rule #4: Since equipment can be large, find pieces that are right for the size of the room. It is acceptable to have one giant piece of equipment in a small room as long as the room is devoted to this one piece. Try to balance the size of the equipment with the scale of the room and place the exercise pieces where they can be accessed most efficiently.

Rule #5: Equipment doesn't have to be placed in a particular position but it does have to be harmonious with your workout needs. If you require a television in the workout room try to place it so you can both see the door and the television. Also it is nice to have a view out a window. This allows the eyes to focus on more distant objects and keeps them from getting tired.

Rule #6: Safety first. Keep clutter to a minimum. Nothing sets back a workout schedule like an injury. Keeping a clutter–clear space will help prevent accidents.

Rule #7: Clear the energy of the room often. Many people release their daily stress during workout sessions. In Feng Shui we understand that stress can leave the body and settle into a space. After a while, this negative *Qi* can build up in the room; the space should be cleared regularly or else you may suffer ill effects. (See Clearing a Space, pp. 133).

Media Rooms

The media room is an alternative space I am seeing more and more often. It is usually a room devoted to the television and stereo. A media room is the only room that can be painted entirely black and still attract positive *Qi* (more about this later). While the walls of a media room do not have to be painted black or even a dark color, they should be painted a solid color and there should be no pictures, no art or any other décor that distracts from the focal point of the television screen.

Having a separate media room does make watching television a special experience. It also makes it difficult to spend too much time watching the television because in the typically dark media room, there is not much else one can do other than watch the screen. If the room is the center of a variety of different activities it is not really a media room but a family room. (See Chapter 5, Family Rooms, pp. 79.) Media rooms have a few special rules for placing furniture.

Rule #1: In a media room it is acceptable for people to sit with their backs to the door. Most media rooms have a large television which acts as a mirror, so it is possible to observe what is going on behind you. Also, media rooms are often furnished with high–backed chairs which can shield from the negative *Qi* normally created by sitting with one's back to the door.

Rule #2: It is perfectly suitable to paint your media room entirely black. The color black actually lends itself to the theater–like quality people are trying to achieve in this type of room thus adding to the enjoyment of the media experience. In other words, black walls are in harmony with the purpose of the room and therefore good Feng Shui. Rooms that are all black have a lot of power; the energy is both compelling and protective at the same time. As long as the room is only used for short periods, the color black is a fine choice.

Meditation Rooms

Many of my clients these days either have a meditation room or are in the process of creating one. This room is specifically devoted to prayer, journaling, meditation and sometimes yoga.

This room should be a sanctuary where only the most positive *Qi* is allowed entry and encouraged to stay. It should be a special place where you can go to shut out the world and commune with your spiritual self. Here are a few guidelines for setting up a meditation room:

Start with a clean, energetically clear room. At the beginning, remove everything from the room, then clean the room thoroughly. Clean the carpet or floors and wash down the walls with a solution of baking soda and vinegar (if you have never used baking soda and vinegar, be warned! There will be lots of fizz when you mix them, but they make a very safe cleaning combination.)

Consider painting the walls in colors you really like. Meditation rooms do not have to be purple or lavender, though this palette is conducive to meditation and spiritual work. If you love yellow, paint it yellow or decorate with shades of yellow. If you love red, choose red as your color theme. Choose a color that excites you, that feels inviting to you, one that makes you want to go into the room, sit down and spend time.

Clean the furniture you are going to place in the room. As you clean the items, you will be clearing them energetically as well.

Add protection symbols to three sides of the room. This room needs to feel like a sanctuary, so it deserves additional protection. Place protective symbols on each of the walls, except for the wall that holds the door you will use to enter the space. Protective symbols can be religious symbols (icons, angels, saints, statues, etc.) or Feng Shui cures (dragons, foo dogs, bamboo plants, mirrors, etc.).

Make "knock first" a rule for this room. This is your space, and you have a right to spend time in it, uninterrupted. Set a boundary, then enforce it.

Finally, if you use this room daily, energetically clear the room about once a month. This is the room where you will spend time casting off the trouble and stress of your days. So, every once in a while, you want to clear the room and refresh and re–circulate the Qi. Clear the room with sound (bells), salt or smudge. (See Clearing a Space, pp. 133 for more information.)

Studios

A studio is similar to a craft room, except that it is used for professional purposes. Because you are trying both to be creative and to attract business it is very important to keep the entryways clear. The main door to the room should not be blocked in any way and should be able to swing fully open. This will allow business as well as creative ideas to flow in.

Another important consideration is how this studio space connects your life to your life's work. You are fortunate to have found something you love to do—and you are either already making a living at it or in the process of doing so. Consider that your studio is the "heart" of your life's work. Keep it clean, organized and well lit (if appropriate). Make it a room you long to spend time in, and it will reward you by supporting your efforts and bringing you success in all your endeavors.

Sunrooms

Sunrooms are wonderful rooms—not really porches—but enclosed areas suitable for use during three or four seasons. Since this is a family area, the rules about clutter, furniture placement and décor for living areas all apply. By definition, a sunroom has lots of windows and natural light and therefore it attracts a lot of *Qi*. Often a sunroom can be the most–used room of the house. Sunrooms are excellent places to work on creative projects— especially painting, writing, drawing and sewing. Sunrooms are also an excellent place to study or meditate.

Workshop

A workshop is a craft room with heavy equipment; and usually more dust and debris. Workshops are often located in basements, out–buildings or garages. For these reasons organization and neatness help keep the space accident–free. It is important to create a system for maintaining tools in good working order and to keep projects organized.

If you spend long hours in a workshop and you are working with precise equipment, it is best to work facing the door. You don't want to be startled by someone coming in—it might cost you a fine piece of wood, or worse, cause a physical injury. If you must work with your back to the door, install a bell or flashing light that signals when someone has entered. This will allow you to concentrate fully on what you are doing even when family members decide to pop in unannounced.

Storage Areas

Technically storage areas have little or no *Qi* because they are usually dark, cluttered areas where little circulation or movement occurs. When storage areas are used for storage, the stuff does not require a lot of *Qi* movement, and the quality of any *Qi* in the area is not important to the articles stored there. However, if you are using your home's storage areas as living spaces, the quality and movement of the *Qi* becomes an important issue. For instance, if your finished basement is being rented out to your nephew, re-read the section on Guest Bedrooms in Chapter 6 to see tips on décor and furnishing. If your attic doubles as your home office, check the section in this chapter on Home Offices for some tips on desk placement, etc. But if you are truly using your storage areas for storing items, there are just a few things to consider.

Attics

Being from the West Coast, where usable attic spaces were mostly non–existent, I was shocked and pleasantly surprised to find livable attics galore in New England. This makes up for, in my opinion, the tiny, tiny closets New Englanders seem to accept without complaint. Here are a few rules for attics:

Rule #1: Have good lighting. If you use your attic, good lighting is a must. This will help keep accidents to a minimum—and light helps bring *Qi* into the space.

Rule #2: Keep pests out whenever possible, this includes bats, rats, bugs, and birds. The bat and cricket are both considered lucky; the rat is the first symbol of the Chinese Zodiac (he is also hardworking and detail oriented); and the bird attracts happy relationship *Qi*—but none of these should make its home in your attic. By all means, let your son have a pet rat, give your daughter her own ant farm, attach a bat house to an exterior wall of your house, put out a bird feeder or have pet birds in the house—all are excellent ways to attract positive *Qi*. But pests are pests and not good energy for your attic.

Rule #3: If someone in the house is recovering from an illness they should not sleep under heavily cluttered areas of the attic. Shift attic contents so the person convalescing is not directly under the clutter. If this is not possible, move attic contents so they are evenly distributed throughout the space.

Basements

Basements are another space most people on the West Coast are not familiar with. However, my own grandmother, who lived in an old Spanish–style home in the Larchmont district of Los Angeles did have a basement. I remember it as being a mysterious place, filled with old trunks, boxes and a monstrous, brown furnace—nothing like my basement today which is at ground level, open and bright with high ceilings. I love basements and wish everyone had one as nice as the one I have today. While all of the rules pertaining to attics—with regard to lighting and pests—apply to basements, there are just a couple more things to keep in mind.

It is acceptable to clutter up a basement. It is meant as a place for storage and so it is ideal to keep your stuff there. Of course, if you have so much stuff that you hate going down into your basement and you feel overwhelmed at the prospect of hunting for your Christmas lights, it is time to do some sorting.

It is perfectly fine to sleep above the basement no matter how much stuff is stored in it. Sleeping under attic clutter is not good because it can feel "uncomfortable" to have all of that heavy Qi trapped by the clutter pressing down on you. This is not the case with a basement, since you are lying on top of the collection of possessions you have stored there.

Watch out for mold. Mold is a serious health concern and can affect the well–being of everyone in the house. It can also affect the prosperity and the future (not to mention property values) of the house itself. If you suspect you have mold growing in your basement, bring in a professional and get rid of it.

Closets

Feng Shui guidelines for closets are fairly clear: "If there is clutter in your home, best to hide it in a closet." Closets do not attract Qi and therefore, if they are cluttered, the energy of the home will not be affected the same way as it is when clutter is in the living spaces. On the other hand, it is certainly not any fun to open a closet door and have the contents fall out onto the floor; nor do you want a closet that is so filled and crowded with your own or the family's possessions that half of the contents needs to be removed in order for anyone to be able to access the vacuum cleaner. While closets don't need to be clutter–free, they do need to be accessible, and you do need to be able to easily find and use your possessions.

Rule #1: Make sure the closet door closes properly. In general, doors that don't close properly affect the family structure and the family standards (family in this instance means the family you live with—including your pets). When the improperly closing doors are closet doors, argumentative energy will be found in the home. If it is just a matter of trying to contain too many possessions in the closet, there is an easy remedy: garage sale. But, if there is something structurally wrong with the door that prevents you from being able to close it, have it looked at by a professional.

Rule #2: Watch out for "bad bite" closet doors. Closet doors across from other doors can bring challenges to the flow of the *Qi* in the house; these closet doors can create "bad bites." This is because closet doors are often smaller than regular doors—these mismatched doors are called "bad bites" and cause the people living in the house to feel irritable and stressed. (For more information on bad bites, see the section on Hallways on page 122.)

Though I have already indicated that a cluttered closet is, for the most part, acceptable, I need to add one caveat. If you start to feel emotionally "stuck" in your life, cleaning out a cluttered closet can be very emotionally purging. Clearing out or cleaning out a closet is one of those physical actions that creates an emotional change. If you feel that you are carrying an emotional burden you just cannot seem to let go of, try cleaning out a few closets and see if you do not feel a renewed sense of personal energy and an increased interest in the world around you.

The above pertains to almost all of the closets in the house— with the exception of the closet by the front door. This closet should be entirely free of clutter for two reasons. First, it is the one seen by guests. And second (and more importantly) the front door is the one which allows all new *Qi*, new opportunities and new money to enter your life. You want the area around the front door to be as clear as possible. Of all of the closets in the house, make the one by the front door the most organized, the cleanest and the most usable.

Garages

Whether you have an attached garage or a separate building, you may find you have one of three types of situations: your garage is a place for storing stuff and your car(s); your garage is a active work area; or your garage has been remodeled into an office, playroom, bedroom, etc. If your garage is converted space, you don't actually have a garage and should follow the rules and guidelines outlined for that particular type of room.

This leaves us with two types of garage spaces. Let us begin with an analysis of the storage type. A standard garage usually contains a vehicle or two, tools, the lawn mower and a wide variety of collected and stored possessions. Sometimes people maintain the neatest garage imaginable (I have even seen carpeted ones), so their car(s) "sleep" in a room as nice as anyone's in the family. Yet, while maintaining a clutter–free environment is always good, it is still quite difficult to attract positive *Qi* into a room basically used for storage. For this reason, any cures you place in your garage don't really have much of an effect on the people who live in the house. But you can add protection cures to protect the contents of the garage. Protection cures range from power animals, to mirrors, to even weapon–like tools. Place the cures to the left or right of the exterior entrance(s) to the garage.

Try not to over–clutter your garage. A filled garage is no fun to clean and the things inside are not benefiting you or your family if they are hidden away and covered with cobwebs. When a garage is attached to the house and contains too much stuff, the people living in the house have reduced their ability to be mobile and flexible in life. On the other hand, when the garage is free standing from the house, all of the possessions in it feel disconnected from us (the same goes for items stored off your property at a storage facility). These items become like an anchor we are dragging around through life, not benefiting anyone in the family. When we have too much stuff we can become stuck.

Once the garage is full, then it starts to overflow into the house. There it can actually cause health problems. If you have a problem getting to the boxes in your garage, the Feng Shui suggestion is to clear the space first energetically, then begin to clear it out physically. Clearing the *Qi* will help remove your attachment to the objects so that you can see them more objectively and decide what is really worth keeping. (See the section on clearing a space on page 133.)

Because garages attract so little energy on their own, the room above the garage can be affected. When the garage is attached to the house, the house itself will usually provide enough *Qi* even for the rooms over the garage. But if the garage is detached from the main house and there is a room or rooms above (usually occupied by an adult child or in–law, and sometimes rented out), occupants of that room will receive so little Qi that they may find it difficult to pursue their lives and their goals. Often times they will need to place additional cures to bring positive energy to their lives. Wind chimes and bells are the best cures and can be hung outside the door to their room(s). The Qi needs to find its way up the stairs and into the residence—and it will need lots of coaxing along the way. Consider hanging or adding as many as three or four cures to really stimulate the flow of the Qi.

If your garage serves as the main entrance to the house, and if all of your comings and goings are through that one giant door, you are not energizing your home's front door, and you are missing opportunities. All new opportunities enter into your life through your front door. The Qi that comes into your home through your garage door carries the same energy you have now and nothing more (and probably less because the energy is weakened by clutter in the garage.) Try to use your front door at least once a week, more often if possible. (For more information on this, see Front Entryways, pp. 53.)

Junk Room

If you have a junk room, you are already in trouble. This is a room that could be your study, your meditation room, your craft room—but it has simply become a dumping ground for stuff you have no immediate interest in using. My suggestions for this stuff are: donate it, sell it, trash it. Do not keep stuff you perceive as useful, keep only the stuff you use. Clear out the room now, so that additional beneficial Qi, fresh, exciting money opportunities and new, happy relationships can come into your life. Do not waste part of your precious home storing stuff you don't like and don't use.

What if you have a "junk drawer"? You know, a drawer in the where you put the spare batteries, pens, matches and maps—that is just fine. But try to keep this type of storage limited to one or two drawers maximum.

To get rid of junk, find some clean new cardboard boxes. Place junk inside the box. On the outside of the box, write an inventory list of everything that is in the box. Then put the date on the box and seal it. Leave it in the junk room. If in four to six weeks (or in

Moving Energy Through Hallways

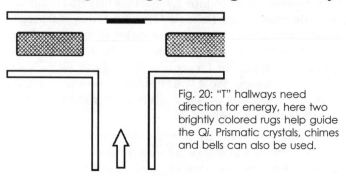

Fig. 20: "T" hallways need direction for energy, here two brightly colored rugs help guide the Qi. Prismatic crystals, chimes and bells can also be used.

Fig. 21: "L" hallways also need help guiding the Qi. Here attractive, colorful pictures are hung to give interest and energy after the turn in the hall.

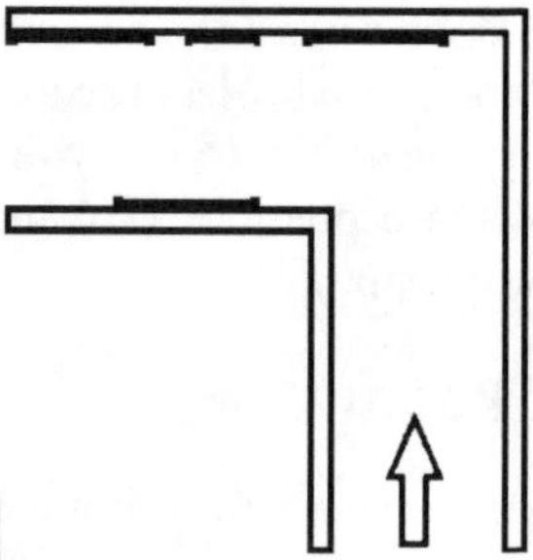

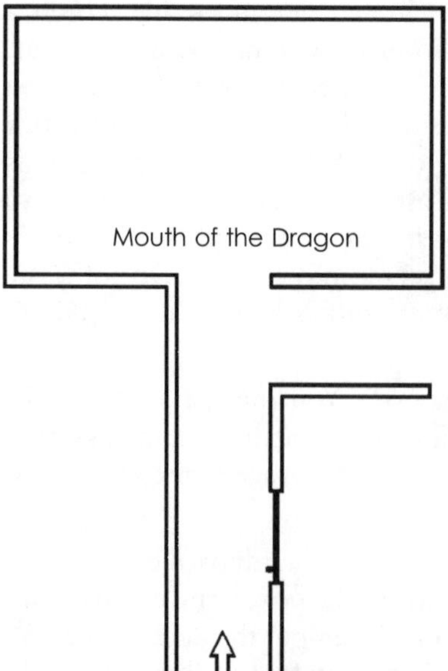

Mouth of the Dragon

Fig. 22: A room at the end of a long hall is called the "mouth-of-the-dragon." The occupant of this room can seem hostile and uncooperative or wield great power. Rooms like this are ideal for bosses and parents but if a child resides in this room there will be a power struggle. The solution is to balance the energy of the east–azure dragon with the west–white tiger. So a picture of a tiger or statue of a tiger in the room will give balance.

a few months for seasonal items), no one in the family has opened the box, then obviously no one needs those items. You can safely donate them to charity without having to re–open the box.

Pantries

Often times pantries are not separate rooms but simply closets specifically intended for food storage. Because items that nourish the family are stored in these spaces, they deserve special attention. And these are very important areas if you are dieting. Here are some ideas to consider:

Have a good supply of ingredients on hand. If we cook and prepare our own meals for ourselves and our family, the food will be prepared with love and will support the wellness of each member of the family. This creates good health Qi and better food energy overall. And we are more likely to cook if there is a ready supply of the ingredients we use.

Discard out–of–date items.

Donate items you will just never use. If canned lima beans were on sale and you bought a number of cans but your family hates canned lima beans—it is probably time to find a charity and donate the beans to someone who does want them.

If you are on a special diet, one designed to help you feel better, to be healthier, or to be trimmer—remove all foods that do not support this goal. Since the whole family will benefit from more healthful eating, simply remove the unhealthy junk food from the pantry altogether. You will not be denying them; you will actually be educating their taste buds now so that they can enjoy a better, healthier future. Junk food, just like junk scattered around the house, merely creates clutter and blocks the flow of Qi. Your body certainly does not need "clutter."

Maintain a balance of items in your pantry. There should be items that satisfy the five tastes: sweet, salty, sour, bitter and astringent. We in the West tend to gravitate toward the first two taste groups only, while in the East, people are more likely to eat a balanced diet including each of the five tastes. Balance creates harmony in the body.

Transitional Areas

These areas are important because they allow us to move from one place to another in our homes. These areas also encourage the Qi to flow throughout the house. Transitional areas can be tricky as they are usually high traffic areas and can therefore become the biggest disrupters of the flow of balanced Qi. Their design is usually unyielding and fixed in the architecture of the home, and yet they can affect the energy of everyone living in the house and of the entire house itself.

Hallways

Hallways are the necessary link between rooms. They connect the public living areas with the private quarters of a house. However, hallways are also where Qi most often gets stuck, shattered and diffused, leaving the family with some parts of their lives working well, and others not functioning well at all. Remember, when dealing with hallways, we are trying to pull the Qi from the main entrance or front door into the private quarters of each family member.

Often Qi gets stuck trying to go around a corner. An individual might be able to go down the hall from the living room to their bedroom, making a sharp turn in the hallway on their way. Unfortunately, Qi cannot readily follow the same pathway. Qi tends to move in a straight line until encounters an obstacle and then, if we don't provide a way for it to change directions, it basically stops at the first corner it comes to. Qi needs something at the end of a hallway to help move the energy around the corner (see fig. 20). Here are some ideas that help to move the Qi down past the elbow of your hall.

1. Bounce the energy around the corner using shiny objects. Think of a laser–light beam of Qi shining down your hallway. If it hits a reflective surface, like a mirror, it will bounce directly back in the direction from which it came. But if it hits a reflective surface that is convex, shaped like the back of a spoon, the energy will change directions. So, consider having a large brass bowl or silver–colored plant holder at the end of your T– or L–shaped shaped hallway.

2. Bounce the energy around the corner using objects made of cut–glass. Crystal vases and cut–glass chandeliers all bounce light around. Each facet of the glass is reflective and sends the energy in all different directions. This helps Qi move along the pathway and into other spaces.

3. The quickest way to move energy around is with a prismatic crystal. This cut glass crystal, sometimes called an Austrian crystal, is designed to reflect light into tiny rainbows. Try to incorporate the crystal into your overall décor. It is not helpful to simply dangle a single prismatic crystal out in space. It looks odd and therefore does not attract positive Qi. Instead, try to have the crystal form part of a light fixture, or hang it from one of the branches of a plant as a kind of decoration. I have seen some very beautiful angel statues where the angel was depicted holding a bowl and a crystal had been placed in the bowl. I have seen a nice arrangement of pictures held up by ribbons— at the top of each ribbon was a prismatic crystal. Try to be creative and blend your cures seamlessly into the design and décor of your home.

4. Move Qi in a new direction by placing objects off–center. An object or picture placed off–center will attract attention and energy and bounce it off in a different direction. Place wall sconces on either side of a painting. Or, hang pictures in the hallway where they can be seen as you move down the hallway (see fig. 21).

Another problem with some hallways is that the bend or turn can create a "poison arrow" (a protruding corner). If the corner points into a room it can create very disruptive energy, energy that causes unrest and arguments. It can bring residents in the house illness, low energy levels and lack of motivation. The individual residing or spending time in the room at which the poison arrow points will spend most of their strength fighting the arrow and have little left for living successfully in the world. Correcting a poison arrow is easy and makes a big difference in the flow of energy, and the overall feeling of satisfaction in a house. Here are some tips for neutralizing a poison arrow in your home:

Neutralize a poison arrow by hanging a string of bells from the ceiling in front of the corner. You don't have to cover the entire corner, but the lowest bell should hang at least at eye level for the person whose room the poison arrow is invading. In other words, if your son or daughter occupies the room under attack from the poison arrow, then the bells need only hang down as far as his or her eye level (and can be adjusted upwards as they grow into their full height).

You could hang a plant (silk or live) to block the negative *Qi* that results from a poison arrow. The plant need not cover the whole corner, but it is good if the tendrils of the plant hang down to eye level. You could also place a plant on a stand in front of the corner if the hallway is large enough to accommodate it.

You can hang fabric, (or even a table runner)—anything that will soften the corner will help to neutralize the bad *Qi*.

You can use mirrors to neutralize the poison arrow. This is my least favorite cure because I think it looks a bit odd—and that alone can disrupt the *Qi* in your home. On the other hand, it's best to have all the options. Take two very small mirrors (less than two inches in diameter) and place one on each side of the corner up where the wall meets the ceiling. This is not as attractive an option as hanging bells or fabric but it is very effective.

Whether your hall is T–shaped or L–shaped or just a plain straight line, if it ends at a door, this doorway is called the "mouth–of–the–dragon"—just by the sound of it, you probably know that this is not a lucky circumstance (see fig. 22). Dragons may represent something very powerful, something that captures one's imagination—but walking into a dragon's mouth is never a good thing.

If the door at the end of your hallway is a closet or utility room, no problem; if it is a bathroom, members of the family may develop intestinal problems; if it is a study or an office, the person who uses this room could tend to isolate themselves from the family and may "bite people's heads off" if they enter unannounced; if it is a guest room, you could find yourself with a really unruly guest on your hands; if it is your room, you may appear to be unapproachable to others living in the house. And, if it is a child's room, well, you may just have one very angry, snarling, fire–breathing, scary little person, much like a dragon–in–training, stomping around the house. To solve this problem, Feng Shui utilizes the wisdom of the Chinese Zodiac.

In the Chinese Zodiac the symbol of the dragon sits opposite the tiger—the dragon represents Yang energy and the Tiger, Yin energy. The tiger helps balance the dragon. To add a tiger to this area, you might choose a picture of a tiger and hang it to one side of the door. You could add a statue of a tiger near the entrance to the room so that it would be the first thing you see when you enter the space. You could even add a cuddly, stuffed tiger to the bed, facing the door. This will help diffuse the negative power of the "mouth–of–the–dragon."

If the *Qi* in your home moves through several doorways before reaching the "mouth–of–the–dragon," the person residing in that room will be quite a handful to live with. The trapped energy will build to an unbearable level inside the room, making the occupant irritable, angry and even violent. If you are experiencing tendencies like these from a person residing in such a room, add metal to the room. Metal will help cut the strong dragon energy in two, thus curbing the person's power and anger. You may choose to add metal furniture, pictures in metal frames—or prominently display metal art in the room.

The longer or darker the hallway, the more difficult it is for the *Qi* to move through it. If *Qi* doesn't move, it will not reach the rooms connected by the hall. For very dark halls, try adding lamps, sconces or ceiling lights and keep the lights on during the day. If adding lights is impractical, consider hanging a collection of mirrors on the wall which will reflect light and brighten up the area.

If the hallway consists of a series of doors, one door after another that order to proceed down the hall, *Qi* will end up moving very quickly. *Qi* that moves too quickly will cause the people who live in the house to argue and experience stressful relations with one another (and with people outside the home). It is best to slow down the *Qi*.

The cure for this is to place plants along its path. If there is space, add plants to tables positioned along the sides of the hallway. This will help calm the *Qi* and encourage it to become healing and helpful to the people in the house.

If there is not enough room for plants or tables with plants, try hanging some bells. These can be hung over pictures or above doorways (high enough to allow the doors to close). As the *Qi*

Bad Bites In Hallways

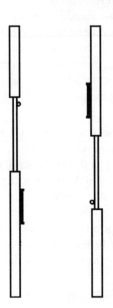

Fig. 23: A bad bite is when two doors in a hall do not line up exactly opposite each other. As shown here the two doors across from each other are slightly askew and this causes the Qi to be blocked. The family will experience arguing, disagreements over small things and a general lack of harmony in the house. The solution is to balance out the hallway with reflective energy, in this case, hang pictures (framed with glass in front) beside each door. This will help move the Qi more harmoniously.

Fig. 24: When two doors are mismatched in size, such as a smaller closet door and a wider bedroom door, it creates an energy problem. We still want to move the energy around with reflective objects but here we place them both opposite the larger door. This will allow the Qi to move and flow and the family will have more peace.

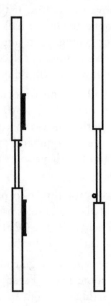

rushes by, it will move through the bell and become harmonious. (See Sound Cures pp.163.)

You can break up the speedy flow of Qi by placing a series of rugs, spaced with gaps between them, so the color beneath your feet changes every yard or so.

Slow the Qi down by hanging framed paintings. Paintings are usually not framed with glass, so they will absorb Qi rather than increase it and speed it along. The colorful paintings will catch the eye, slowing you down, right along with the Qi.

Now, let us consider doors along a hallway that face one another. The purpose of a hallway is to connect rooms, but if the doors in the hall are out of line, (i.e. not directly opposite each other), it can create what is called a "bad bite" (see fig. 23). If two doors are opposite each other, but one door is smaller than the other, Qi cannot travel easily from the larger door to the smaller door (see fig. 24). This also results in the energy–jarring bad bite. In other words, when doors do not match, Qi gets bumped around. This results in family members arguing with one another, poor health and general irritation.

The bad bite is a fairly common problem with hallways. Most closet doors are smaller than room doors, causing a problem. Double doors for laundry closets are much larger than doors to the rooms, creating another problem. And sometimes we find bedroom doors offset. This can cause a lot of difficulty between the people who live in those rooms.

The solution for a bad bite is to, in effect, increase the size of the smaller door. This can be done with Feng Shui cures. One way is to hang a picture on either side of the smaller door. Have pictures framed with glass in front so they are reflective. The pictures can be small or large but they should be a balanced pair. I know this may seem confusing. This is one of those things that takes hours to explain and seconds to show. See the diagrams on the facing page.

Staircases

I love a house with stairs, given a choice I always choose a house with stairs. The main issue from a Feng Shui perspective is to find a way to encourage Qi to travel up a staircase in order to circulate in the rooms on the upper levels and to keep it from traveling down the staircase too quickly. You need to be aware that since it is easier to go down stairs than it is to go up, special measures will need to be taken to make sure the flow of Qi remains balanced.

Rule #1: *A staircase should have regular treads and risers.* I know this sounds obvious but I have been to many houses were the steps of the staircase were not even. This can cause accidents, back problems and general stress.

Cure: Rebuild the staircase as required. (Sorry, no easy cure here.)

Example: One of the houses my husband and I have owned had been on the market in Albuquerque for almost a year at the time we purchased it. The main reason it was on the market so long was that the first step of the staircase was ten inches high and the remaining steps were seven inches. This meant that every time you came down the stairs, you landed on the first level floor with a "clunk" because it was difficult for the body to accommodate the extra three–inch height of the bottom step. And you either tripped starting up the stairs, not expecting such a high rise or, slammed your foot down on the second step which was three inches lower than you had expected. So, of course, the house didn't sell. After moving in, we immediately rebuilt the staircase. This balanced out the flow of Qi throughout the entire house, making it one of our favorite places to have lived.

Rule #2: *The more difficult the staircase (staircases with narrow treads or steep climbs), the more difficult it will be to encourage Qi to go up.* Or, perhaps the stairwell is dark and narrow or it turns awkwardly, leaving no step where you expected one. If your house is not blessed with a grand, easy staircase, there are cures.

Cure: Qi can be coaxed up a difficult staircase by placing a "reward" at the top. Place plants, lights, crystals or pictures of living things at the top of the stairs. Use attractive, colorful objects or things that reflect light such as, lights, prismatic crystals, candles and lanterns. Don't place a mirror at the head of the stairs because it will send Qi right back down.

Rule #3: *Corkscrew staircases are usually frowned upon in Feng Shui* because the symbolism of a corkscrew drilling its way through your house does not represent good Qi. Additionally, they are not the easiest of staircases to navigate—especially when you are carrying the laundry or other things up or down the stairs.

Cure: It is less objectionable if your corkscrew staircase is a secondary staircase in the house, and is used by young, energetic teenagers—but, if it is your one and only staircase, you may want to consider changing it in favor of a more conventional style. In the case of loft apartments where this type of staircase is the only one in the home, consider placing a small wine cabinet near the base of the staircase. Fill it with wine bottles or mineral water if you prefer. This will give the corkscrew a useful task rather than metaphorically screwing a hole into the foundation of your family and personal relationships.

Rule #4: Very steep staircases can be a problem.

Cure: Make sure the staircase is very well lit—light attracts *Qi* and will help pull it up even a very steep staircase. Place an attractive painting or some flowers at the top of the stairs to reward the *Qi* when it finally does arrive at the top. Do not place a mirror at the top of a staircase or you will simply (and immediately) send the *Qi* back downstairs. The results of such a mirror placement often manifest in the members of the household working very hard, yet never getting the results they want from the investment of their time and effort. (Symbolically, *Qi* hits the mirror after the difficult climb upstairs and immediately shoots back down; all your work brings nothing in return.)

Rule #5: Narrow staircases choke the Qi. The wider the staircase, the more *Qi* is able to flow smoothly both up and down.

Cure: It is best to light narrow staircases well and even paint them light colors to help the *Qi* flow up and down the stairs.

Rule #6: Staircases with built in obstacles challenge the Qi. Staircases with "disappearing" steps (due to a sharp turn), very low ceilings or other obstacles (that require a warning to visitors) also disrupt the flow of *Qi*.

Cure: Make whatever changes you can. Apply slip–proof treads to the smaller steps and paint low ceilings with bright colors (or use reflector tape) so that accidents can be avoided.

Rule #7: Staircases should not face the front door. Staircases that face the front door cause your luck to run out. Many house styles, especially split levels and Capes, will often have a staircase that points to the front door. This is a real problem when the bottom step of the staircase is directly lined up with the threshold of the door. However, if you have to turn after having entered your front door in order to reach the stairs, your circumstances are somewhat ameliorated because *Qi* tends to move in a straight line; it will be more difficult for it to escape through the doorway.

Cure: If *Qi* is running out your door, you may experience opportunities that come into your life then go before you can grasp them and take advantage of them. Perhaps you are told about an opportunity at work, a new job opening up; but before you can submit your application someone else is chosen to fill the position. Or, you are introduced to an attractive single but by the time you have the courage to ask them out, they are already involved with someone else. To stop the fleeing *Qi*, place a mirror above the front door and send the *Qi* back up the stairs before it can escape. Choose a decorative mirror, however not so large that people can see themselves in it as they walk down the stairs. The mirror should be less than ten inches across. Find a mirror that has a nice, large decorative border—of a size proportional to the space above your front door—or use a very small mirror, less than two inches in diameter, surrounded by some silk flowers or attached to a small plaque. Be creative; try to find a solution that is in harmony with your overall décor. (See pp. 147 for more information on the various types of mirrors.)

If you don't want to place a mirror above your front door, you can place a plant at the bottom of the stairway to either side. The plant, live or silk, will help the *Qi* to pool at the base of the staircase, not leave the house. If there is enough room on the staircase, you can place several small plants on the steps themselves. This will both help *Qi* to move up the staircase and prevent it from running back down.

If the stairs point to the front door but they are very far from the door (15 feet or more), the danger of *Qi* leaving the house is not as great. However, it is still important to protect the flow of *Qi* within your home. Place furniture, plants or lights between the staircase and the front door to help hold the *Qi* in the house.

Rule #8: Broken steps—indoors our out, in living areas or storage areas—are unacceptable. Not only can they lead to injuries, they also severely interrupt the flow of *Qi* from here to there;

metaphorically they disturb the process of your life movement from the present into the future. This affects career success and can block promotions for the members of the household.

Cure: Keep all steps and staircases in good repair.

There is no benefit to having one material on the stairs over another, as long as people feel safe climbing up or down the stairs. Stairs can be wooden or carpeted, they can have rubber treads or be made of stone or metal. All are fine if the stairs themselves are comfortable and reliable for people to use. Glass stairs, which are growing in popularity, are also fine, as long as they feel secure to the user. It doesn't matter if the stairway is open or closed, as long as the individual steps feel safe. Overall, it just important to have a staircase that your family and guests feel comfortable using.

Doors and Windows

We have covered a considerable amount of information about doors and windows in the specific chapters on the rooms of the house.

The door to your home is considered a "mouth" inhaling to bring in Qi from the outdoors and into your home environment. Simply by using the door on a regular basis, you enhance its ability to bring energy into your life and the lives of those who dwell in the home.

The front door brings in new, fresh Qi: opportunities you might want, but were not expecting. If you are looking for a new career or a new relationship, work with a variety of Feng Shui options to enhance the flow of Qi in through the front door.

The back, side and garage doors bring in Qi as well, but this is familiar energy, the types of things that support the life you already are living. If you are trying to stabilize your current job or improve your current relationship, enhance the flow of Qi through the doorway most commonly used by members of your family.

The back door will never attract new Qi, new energy. Just as we rarely invite strangers to enter our home through the back door, fresh Qi cannot find its way to the back door and into our lives to bring promotions at work, pregnancy or new, creative ideas.

A serious problem is that most people who have a side or garage door tend to use it exclusively, rarely using the front door. They are spending a lot of effort on doing things and focusing on activities that are already in place—and not a lot of energy on the new things and opportunities that could enrich their lives. So, try to get into a new habit of using your front door at least once per week.

To enhance the beneficial *Qi* in our lives, we can also hang cures near a door. Many of these are described in detail in the section on cures in this book. However, here are a few additional tips:

Clean the front door regularly, both the glass and the wood. Polish the handle, too. Do this about once a month when you are really trying to attract new opportunities.

Clean the back door when you are trying to finish projects. Make sure the doorway is clear of clutter and that any steps are in good repair.

Consider painting your main door to attract new energy into your life. Red is considered the luckiest of colors and brings bright, happy energy. Or, consider a blue door—it is said that an evil ghost cannot pass through a blue door.

The door itself should be in good repair—closing properly without making any annoying squeaking sounds. If the door does not close properly, it is said that the structure of the family will suffer. It is also said that if you have a noisy door the neighbors will talk about you.

Windows are the "nose" of a house—how it exhales. In the past, having too many windows (more than three per room) was considered bad for prosperity, as all your heat (and therefore, your money) would leak out all of those windows. But, with today's building standards and the high tech, double–pane, insulated glass windows, you can have as many windows as you like without fear of losing wealth.

In some of the traditional teachings of Feng Shui, doors are said to represent the "parents" of the house and windows are the "children." If the doors are small and the windows are very grand, then the children living in the house will be rebellious. Ideally the doors and windows of a home should be in proportion to one another to create balance within the family.

Clearing a Space

There are a couple of Feng Shui techniques for clearing out old energy from a space. Here are some ideas:

Use sound. Ring a bell very loudly around the objects. In effect, you are scaring away the negative and stuck *Qi* (as well as any pests that may be lurking). Ring the bell a few times in each area of the space before moving on to the next. Finish at the main door as though you were ushering out an unwelcome guest.

If your prefer something less noisy, try the method called "Casting Salt". Find some good sea salt (this is available at health food stores or Chinese markets). Sprinkle the salt on the boxes and clutter—even under them if you can. Salt neutralizes *Qi* and helps you release what is no longer necessary to your life.

Try the old–fashioned "move and clean" method. Grab a box or stack of clutter and move it outside. Divide the items into three piles: Keep, Donate and Discard. Your goal should be to have the "Keep" pile as small as possible. Once the box has been sorted and the items in it have been cleared away, head off to the house for another box of stuff. If you do one box every few days, you can be finished with the reorganization of your space in a very short time.

One popular method for clearing energy (Qi) in general is called smudging. Smudging (also known as energetic cleansing) is a Native American technique for clearing a space. I actually wrote a small booklet on the subject years ago which is still a hot little seller.

Here is a condensed description of the process:

Take a small amount of the herb Sage (the same one commonly used every Thanksgiving to spice your turkey stuffing) and place it in a fire–proof dish. Light it with a match or a lighter. Then direct the smudge (the smoke from the burning herb) towards the area or the item you wish to clear energetically. (For more information, see my published work entitled, *"Sage and Smudge, Secrets of Clearing Your Personal Space."*)

Part 2

Part 2

Chapter 8

Cures

The Nine Categories of Cures

There are nine categories of cures and each one has a different use. Some are effective in a variety of different situations while others are used for only very specific purposes. The manner in which we place cures is much like that of the acupuncturist who places healing needles that stimulate the personal Qi energy. If the cure is placed correctly, changes happen quickly; if it is not placed correctly nothing happens or, in rare cases, things can get worse.

However, even with this warning in mind, don't be afraid to experiment—just be aware of your environment and your intuition as you work to balance Qi. Should things take a turn for the worse, simply move the cure. Feng Shui tradition dictates that the placement must be aesthetically pleasing for the cure to be effective. In other words, if the cure doesn't look good, if it looks out of place, or if you are bumping into it or banging your head on it, then your cure is probably in the wrong spot.

Let us preview the nine categories of cures:

Light: Light Cures create light or reflect light. They include lamps, mirrors, candles and crystals. Light cures move Qi, send Qi or, in a few cases, collect Qi. We want to move Qi when things feel slow, when we are searching for opportunities or when we feel we need more focus for activities such as work, housework or creative projects. To "send" Qi means to shift it from one location and direct it to another. Sending Qi is often practiced to protect a house, protect an area of the house or to increase the overall Qi in a specific place. In a few instances we can use a light cure to collect Qi. When Qi is generally lacking in one aspect of our personal environment, we can build Qi by gathering it from other areas where it has accumulated.

Sound: Sound cures make sound. Typical sound cures include bells, chimes and flutes as well as musical instruments of all kinds. In Feng Shui these items are selected and placed in the environment for the specific purposes of harmonizing and calling new, harmonious Qi to a location. Sound cures are used when people feel inclined to fight or disagree or when the Qi itself needs soothing. When choosing sound cures it is important that the sound be pleasing to the people who live in the house, i.e., clanking sounds do not invite harmony.

Living: Living cures include plants and some pets—such as fish and birds (i.e., any living thing that spends the majority of its time in a cage, container or in a specific place). Living cures attract growth Qi; as well as stimulate the overall flow of healthier Qi in the environment/house. This helps not only enhance or improve the physical health of the people who live in the space, but also the health of their relationships and finances. Living cures may be representations or symbols of living things—such as silk plants instead of live plants, animal statues instead of real animals. However, the cure is strongest if it is actually alive.

Moving: Moving cures might be objects such as flags, mobiles, fountains, kites, feathers and fans (both the cooling, oscillating type and the paper, decorative type). Basically anything that does move or could move is a moving cure. These cures cause the Qi to move more rapidly, to circulate beneficial energy throughout a space. Choose this type of cure when the people who live in the space feel tired, disinterested in life or depressed; choose it as well when the house itself feels stale and stagnant. Moving cures can help stimulate activity, interest and energy.

Heavy: Heavy cures are typically things like stone, marble, granite and clay. These cures slow down the flow or movement of Qi, thus stabilizing energy in the environment. If Qi moves too quickly life can become a whirlwind of activity. People who live in the house can experience instability in their jobs, relationships or finances. Heavy objects can anchor or stabilize Qi, creating calm and consistent circumstances. Sometimes heavy objects can be employed as a temporary cure in a home where energy is found to be moving too quickly. Once balance is regained the heavy objects can be put away until needed again.

Scent: Scent cures such as oils, incense and scented candles help clear stagnant energy and attract positive Qi. Scent cures can be used to quickly change and lighten the prevailing energy within a space; or they can be used to "clear" rooms or homes, thus removing negative *Qi*. A house can smell sour due to *sha Qi*; this energy affects the mood of everyone in the house, creating endless discord between them. Scent cures balance *Qi* and bring it back to a positive and harmonious state. If you are sensitive to scent, however, it is recommended that you choose an alternative cure.

Electric/Electronic: Electric/Electronic cures include your television, oscillating fan and computer. These cures stimulate energy and lighten the mood. Too many electric or electronic devices in a space can be distracting, so use them sparingly. In Feng Shui we want to balance the number of electronic devices with the size of the room so that the *Qi* in the space does not become over–stimulated. Living in the modern age as we do, we need to live in harmony with our electronic equipment and devices, so even they have a place in Feng Shui, as an aid to create vibrating energy.

Color: Color offers one of the quickest and easiest ways to change the *Qi* of a room. Each color vibrates creating a specific energy and we are affected by these energy vibrations in a nanosecond. There is much scientific research on the effects of color to our moods and physiology. Color cures can stimulate *Qi*, slow it down or balance it, depending on the color chosen. Color can be added in small amounts to move or change energy in specific places such as adding a certain color to your desk or color can be used throughout the room to call overall good *Qi*. Color cures create change; they call and encourage the flow of *Qi* and are even believed to heal a variety of issues on many levels of the human psyche.

Symbols: The ninth category of cures, symbols, are objects that have a meaning or a story behind them. A symbol attracts similar *Qi* to itself, based on the premise that "like attracts like." Money symbols are thus used to attract wealth, relationship symbols bring opportunities for love, and so on. There are symbols in every culture; since Feng Shui is a Chinese art, we explore a variety of Chinese cultural symbols in this book, suggesting how best to use them to attract specific *Qi* into our lives. When choosing any piece to decorate your home consider what its symbol represents and if that is in harmony with what you want to attract. All the symbols in your home are currently attracting *Qi*, if you are not receiving the help and support you need for your goals, you may want to start by examining the energy you are attracting through the symbols of your knick knacks, art, colors and furniture.

These are the nine categories of Cures. Now we will explore each of the categories in detail.

Chapter 9

Light Cures

Prismatic Crystals

A prismatic crystal is a shaped piece of leaded glass, usually faceted, which is hung from a string or chain (see fig. 25). In the West we most often use these sparkling jewels of glass in beautiful crystal chandeliers. When light hits one of these crystals, it throws off a rainbow of color. The prismatic crystal, especially the round ones, acts as a multitude of tiny mirrors, gently moving Qi and disbursing it throughout the space. The prismatic effect takes Qi and breaks the energy into manageable parts so that Qi is more harmonious and balanced.

While less commonly used in China, prismatic crystals are used almost as much as mirrors in western Feng Shui. The prismatic crystal is extremely effective in moving Qi and blends more easily with Western décor than some of the more traditional cures. Prismatic crystals have several uses and come in a variety of shapes and colors. All of these can be taken into consideration as we choose an appropriate cure.

The most commonly used prismatic crystal is the round one. The shape acts like a collection of small mirror facets, helping move Qi. The octagon attracts beneficial Qi; teardrop shapes ease mourning and are to be used sparingly. Other prismatic crystals are spear–shaped, star–shaped or those that come to a sharp point. These focus Qi very precisely and are generally not an appropriate choice other than in rare instances when they are placed above desks where extreme mental focus is needed for short periods of time. (For example, when it is absolutely necessary to complete the dissertation that is due by the end of the month.)

Prismatic crystals also come in the shape of objects or animals. These are useful as long as the shape or animal is in harmony with the type of Qi you are trying to attract. The little glass bumblebees are cute, but if you are deathly allergic to bee stings you may not want to invite this particular type of Qi into your home. For a list

Prismatic Crystals

Fig. 25: Prismatic crystals are found in many shapes and colors. The principle is that the crystal takes light and breaks it into colors, likewise it takes energy and disburses it into an area or room. Round shapes bring balanced energy while pointed shapes bring more focused energy. Clear crystals bring general energy while different colors focus certain types of energy.

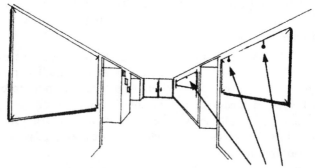

Fig. 26: Crystals can be used to move energy down a long hallway. Ideally the crystals would be hung with art or wall hangings so that the crystal looks like it is part of the décor.

Fig. 27: The crystal can also be hung in areas where you want to have more focus and attention. The crystal, with it's prismatic qualities takes energy and breaks it down into manageable parts, improving concentration and helping you finish important tasks.

of animals and their symbolic meanings see the section on Animal Symbols, pp. 170.

Prismatic crystals come clear and in a variety of colors—clear being the most popular. The clear crystal breaks down light into the colors of the rainbow, putting the benefit of every color's energy at your disposal. Red is the second most popular color and encourages greater focus on a goal as well as good luck in general. Aurora is the name used to describe a crystal which has been dipped in gold; the resulting rainbow effect is on the crystal itself. Aurora crystals are usually more expensive than the plain ones but the effect can be worth the price. Purple is another color sometimes used; it is good for spiritual work but less helpful when you need to circulate grounding Qi, practical Qi, or take care of the physical aspects of your life.

Prismatic crystals have several helpful uses in Feng Shui:

To disburse energy: In some instances Qi, for whatever reason, starts flowing in a single direction when you would prefer that it disburse into several areas. The most common situation is when you have a staircase that is in line with your front door. (In other words, the bottom stair lines exactly with the threshold of the front door.) The Qi of the house barrels down those stairs and directly out your door. The result is that the members of the family perceive that opportunities come and go before they can get a grip on them. For instance, a promotion is promised then retracted before the family member can accept the offer. Or, a female member of the household is introduced to a new man, and both feel an initial attraction. He is handsome, kind and is exactly the type of potential mate the woman has wanted to meet but he gets transferred out of town before she can even get a first date. Or, after a period of physical exhaustion, health and vitality spring back for a day or two, only to disappear again as the old tiredness returns.

To keep good Qi from leaving your house too quickly, hang a prismatic crystal above the inside of your front door. It can be placed there, incorporated into a decorative arrangement, or hung from a light fixture. The crystal will help disburse the entering Qi and keep the existing energy from leaving the house. (Note: If you already have a mirror above the front door, you will not need a crystal.)

To move energy: If you have a long, dark hallway or a hallway that turns, it is necessary to move Qi down that hallway in order for it to reach the rooms along the way. Remember, all Qi enters the house through the front door, and if you want to move it down into rooms along the hallway, you need to give it a little help.

In the case of long dark hallways, prismatic crystals can increase the Qi, so hang one or two in the hallway (see fig. 26). Crystals do not have to be hung in the center of the hallway in order to be effective; indeed, it looks a little odd to have a single crystal dangling from a red string in the middle of a walkway. However, if you do have a dangling crystal, remember that it needs to be hung high enough so the tallest member of the household can walk under it without banging his or her head on it. Consider hanging the crystals from wall sconces or artwork or place them on side tables in the hall. Choose the number of crystals based on the length of the hall (the longer the hallway, the more crystals you will need—one about every four to five feet), but even one will improve the flow of Qi greatly.

If your hallway turns, it may be quite difficult for the Qi to find its way to the rooms at the end of the hall. This can result in a variety of problems including troubled sleep, slow healing, apathy and disinterest in life. A prismatic crystal is the perfect cure to use to encourage the Qi to change directions at the turn in your hallway. The crystal functions the same way a bunch of tiny mirrors would, reflecting the Qi in every direction. Hang the crystal in the corner of the hallway's turn so that the Qi can bounce off the corner itself and continue on its way down the rest of the hallway.

If your hallway ends in a "T" you will also want to bounce the Qi along—this time in both directions. Your crystal should be hung at the top of the "T" because from this vantage point it will disburse the Qi in multiple directions. The crystal can be hung on the wall or away from the wall, as long as it looks appropriate. One of my clients chose to hang her bumblebee crystal over a vase of flowers; it appeared that the bee had found a bouquet buffet. Be creative as you make the crystals a useful and attractive part of your décor.

To focus energy: Sometimes we need to gather our energy and focus for a specific project. Other times we simply need extra energy to carry through the monotony of our daily tasks. In this day and age we seem to have less and less time to take care of ourselves.

Cooking and caring for our bodies is pushed aside as we maintain our busy lives—and our health may suffer for it. Some of our "labor–saving" devices (such as the computer) likely don't save either much labor or time. The prismatic crystal can help you focus on an important aspect of your life, attracting and distributing enough *Qi* to allow you to focus your attention where it is needed.

In this case we hang the crystal in a window near the area where we want to or need to spend time. Hang a prismatic crystal in your kitchen window to bring more *Qi* for preparing and enjoying healthy foods. Hang the crystal in your home office to bring yourself to the computer or work station more often. Hang the crystal over your telephone to bring energy to your sales calls. Hang the crystal over study areas to improve the quantity and quality of study time (see fig. 27).

Candles

Candles have the power to bring *Qi* to a specific area of the house. Candles have been a part of our history going back to the beginning; our ancestors used candles every day of their lives. Candles instantly make us feel warm and cozy and they bring warm, cozy feelings to our homes as well. Candles also—because they should not be left unattended—keep us anchored to an area of the house, and are therefore very useful cures for creating focus and attention.

When considering candles as cures, think about the color, scent and shape of the candle. Candles are light cures, but they can also serve as scent and color cures. (Note: Candles are only light cures if they are lit.) Candles do not need to be burning all the time in your house—a few hours a week will bring in and circulate an abundance of *Qi*.

When choosing candles make sure that the color, scent and shape are in harmony with the type of *Qi* you want to attract (see sections on Color, pp. 206, Scent, pp. 202, and Symbols, pp. 215 for more information.)

Candles have several uses:

To focus energy for a period of time: If you have a project you can't complete (for instance, you are trying to concentrate and everyone and everything around you seems to provide only distractions), lighting a candle may be the perfect solution. Choose a small red or orange candle, usually a column or taper that will burn in just a few hours. Sit at your desk and light the candle. Start work and keep working until the candle goes out by itself. If you do this even just one day a week, you will find that you accomplish more in a month than you have in the previous six excuse–filled months.

To bond family energy: As I mentioned above, our ancestors used to gather around lighted candles or a fire and connect with one another as a family at the end of the day. The same can be true today. So many of us are mesmerized by flame. Take a tray with several pillar candles (usually an odd number, a Yang number) and light the candles. Candles can be sweetly scented (perhaps vanilla or a fruit scent). Even if you start by sitting there alone with a book or craft project, soon other family members will gravitate towards the room to spend time together with you and each other. Remember to extinguish the candles after an hour or two.

To call energy: Since candles bring focus and Qi, we can use them as a point for meditation. A candle can help "send" our wish, prayer or desire out into the Universe, simultaneously calling energy, from the outside to help us reach our goals. When using candles, the color, scent and shape must always be appropriate to the goal. For instance, if you wanted to call more money to your household, you could burn a metallic gold candle. (Gold is the color of large sums of money.) Metallic candles are usually unscented and either a taper (where the candle grows wider as it burns) or a pillar (which denotes strength) would be appropriate choices for such a goal. Sit with the lit candle for a few moments and visualize money and financial benefit flowing towards you from a variety of directions. Spend another hour in the room doing other things as you allow the candle to continue burning. Extinguish the candle before leaving the room and re–light it daily, repeating the process, until the candle is done.

To send energy: Sometimes we want to send Qi to another person—in the form of emotional support or encouragement— because we want to connect with them. If possible, place the person's picture by the candle and let the candle burn for about an hour per evening until it is done. You can also burn additional candles weekly to strengthen the Qi. Choose a candle color that represents the type of Qi you wish to send—red for love, green for health, yellow for joy, etc. (See Color, pp. 206) Choose a pleasant scent (if desired) and shape.

Sometimes we feel sad, angry, frustrated or out of balance because of the actions of others. A message they have communicated to us allows sha Qi to establish itself in our hearts and in our environment. Rather than allowing this negative Qi in our lives we may decide to return it to its source. If returning Qi to another, place a candle near a window facing the direction of his or her house. (For example, if the house is located three states away but that state is to the south of your dwelling, place the candle in a south–facing window.) Choose an appropriate color— black to denote your displeasure with the situation, blue to ask for peace and white to simply return energy. An unscented candle is usually best in this case. Light the candle and sit with it for a few moments, picturing the Qi floating back. Continue to be in the room with the candle for another hour or so, then extinguish it. Repeat this each evening until the candle will no longer light. Toss the leftover wax in a trash can, off your property.

Mirrors

Mirrors, a light cure, are probably the most commonly used cure in Feng Shui. The Chinese have been using mirrors since the first century B.C.E., while mirrors were not widely used in the West until the Renaissance. In the beginning, mirrors were polished brass, then later a sheet of glass coated on the back with silver, then aluminum, producing an image by reflection. Today, few of us can go a whole day without using a mirror. We need them, we depend on them.

Since mirrors arrived on the scene, every culture has believed that, somehow, mirrors have magical powers. Down through the centuries mirrors have been used for protection, to move Qi, and even to act as portals to other worlds. In the West, there is the myth of Narcissus, a man so spellbound by his own reflection in a pool that he actually died, pining away for the beauty he saw. This is an example of how mirrors can trap and hold energy captive. In Africa there is a myth that if one looks into a dark pool, a crocodile can drag one's reflection under water, and the person will die. In this myth, we are reminded of the power of the reflective quality of mirrors. In Europe in olden times, when a person was dying, his family would turn all of the mirrors in the house around to face the walls, so the spirit would not see itself outside the body and leave for good. In our culture, dropping or breaking a mirror is still believed to "cause bad luck."

The Aztecs, it is said, would place a bowl of water with a knife in it by the door; if an intruder saw his reflection in the bowl, it would appear to him as though the knife were running through his head. The intruder would become frightened and flee. Here a mirror is used for protection.

There is the myth of Perseus, the Greek hero, who had to fight the monstrous Medusa. The sight of Medusa's face and curling braids of snakes could turn a man to stone. When forced to encounter Medusa, Perseus took a shield, shiny as a mirror, and fought her while looking only at her reflection. He successfully defeated Medusa. Here, the mirror is used to deflect negativity.

In India, people believed that one could draw down the moon by placing a bowl of water outside so that the moon was reflected in it. The water, now charged with the light of the moon, was given to a sick person to drink in one gulp. In this instance the "mirror" is used to hold energy for healing. In China, the oldest brass mirrors are considered powerful protection. They are called *Gu Tong Jing* and they are said to reveal hidden spirits, they can also be used to predict the future.

In Feng Shui, mirrors are used extensively to move energy, protect an area or to collect *Qi*. The mirror's power is in the reflection and for Feng Shui purposes, a mirror can be anything that produces a reflection, but for this section, we will concentrate on actual mirrors of different sizes, shapes and types.

Mirror Shapes

A variety of mirror shapes can be used as Feng Shui cures. The round shape is one of the most useful, as it represents the energy of heaven. This energy reflects a balanced, harmonious flow of *Qi*. Square– and rectangular–shaped mirrors are quite acceptable and represent earth, a stable and grounded flow of *Qi*. Triangles—a very unusual shape for mirrors—are not used in Feng Shui as the shape is seen as incomplete and the points, too sharp. Polygons of four sides or more may be used, the most auspicious being the octagon (more about that later in the section on *ba–gua* mirrors). Pentagon–shaped mirrors have a balanced energy as the number five represents the five Chinese elements (wood, metal, fire, earth and water), the five virtues, the five senses, the five major organs in the body and so on. Hexagon–shaped mirrors represent the *Qi* of harmony in the family. Nonagon–shaped mirrors represent happiness and longevity *Qi*. The heptagon is generally avoided as the number seven is not considered a lucky number (in Chinese the word for the number seven sounds like the word for a death ritual). Two other shapes should not be used, that of the tombstone (an arched shape that I have found in numerous homes—see fig. 30) and the coffin shape which I have only seen in one dwelling, so far.

Example: I had occasion to visit a lovely, country–style house (with a wonderful large farmer's porch) just last year, and found a pair of tombstone–shaped mirrors in the upstairs bathroom that the daughters in the family shared (see fig. 30). One of the girls, perhaps because of a sibling squabble, had written her name on one of these mirrors in dry–erase pen. In effect, she had written her name on a tombstone. This, as you might guess, is not considered good Feng Shui, or good for the health—so I recommended that not only the name be removed but that the mirrors be replaced with a more acceptable shape.

Basic Rules for Mirrors

Mirrors can be any size, but the rule is if they are large enough to allow a person to see his or her full head, they need to be hung so that the tallest member of the household can see his or her whole head. If the mirror is hung too low and the top of a person's head is "cut off" it is considered bad for his or her health.

If using a smaller mirror, one in which a person cannot see their entire head, placement and use are usually based on the situation. Often, smaller mirrors are used to correct problems, and larger mirrors are used to move Qi.

When choosing a mirror find one with a frame that goes with your décor, or use a frameless mirror. You can use traditional Chinese mirrors which are very effective for some situations. But if the Chinese mirror clashes with your Ethan Allen furniture, your décor is at cross purposes and the mirror will not be effective.

Ba–gua Mirrors

The *ba–gua* mirror is a special mirror used in Feng Shui (see fig. 28). Its distinctive design makes it easy to differentiate between it and other mirrors. It consists of an eight–sided wooden frame holding a small, round mirror. The entire piece usually measures less than six inches across. The frame consists of a design, usually printed on paper, that is red, green and gold. The familiar design consists of the eight trigrams of the *I Ching*, laid out in the "later heaven" sequence. In fact, the word *ba–gua* means "eight symbols of divination"—a reference to the eight trigrams. This special design and mirror combination is used to protect your home. The mirror is placed in the window closest to the front door, facing outside (see fig. 34). It can be hung or set to lean against the window or, it can be taped to the window itself. The story goes that if evil comes to your door it will be drawn to see its face in the mirror, become frightened and run away. But if good comes to the door it will see its reflection and feel welcomed and want to stay.

Example: A few years ago I was called to consult at a one-story adobe–style home with exposed exterior vigas (quite nice) and I was busy installing one of these mirrors in the front window for the client when her husband came home unexpectedly. I explained to him how this would prevent evil from entering the house. He looked at me and said with the straightest of faces, "Well, how am I going to get in?" So, I guess here is a good place to point out that protection cures don't work on the evil that lives in your home. If you have invited the evil into your home and married him or her, you need more than a *ba–gua* mirror—you probably need a lawyer!

If you don't have a window near the front door (many apartments do not) you can place the *ba–gua* mirror in your bedroom window. Again, it needs to be placed facing outside. This type of mirror is never used in the house, but is always set in a window, facing out.

Example: After one of my lectures, a youthful, health–oriented man approached me with a question. It seems he had found a *ba–*

Mirrors

Fig. 28: The *ba–gua* mirror is a protection mirror usually hung in a window facing out. The word *ba–gua* refers to the eight trigrams of the *I Ching: The Chinese Book of Changes* and represents the eight major areas of life. The eight are seen here as lines and dashes surrounding the mirror.

Fig. 29: Convex mirrors, where the mirror in the center is shaped like the back of a spoon, send back energy very aggressively and so are used when protection is greatly needed. On the other hand, concave mirrors, those shaped like a little bowl, collect the *Qi* and are particularly useful if you live in an area that has weak or slow *Qi*, such as a cul–de–sac or dead end street.

Fig. 30: While the octagonal mirror is considered the luckiest, other shapes are fine to use. There are two exceptions. One is the coffin–shaped mirror (quite rare) and the other is the tombstone–shaped mirror (the more common arch shape).

I visited one home with tombstone–shaped mirrors in the kid's bathroom. And one child, probably trying to define her territory, had written her name in dry–erase pen on the mirror thus writing her own name on a graveyard headstone.

gua mirror in Chinatown and, liking the design, had hung it up in his home office (he was a massage therapist). "And your business went through the floor, right?" He agreed that business was very slow. Without knowing it, he had used the mirror to "protect" himself from all of his sad and hurting clients.

The *ba–gua* mirror is also helpful with difficult neighbors. Instead of putting the mirror in your front window, direct the mirror toward the offending neighbor. This will reflect back to them their own behavior. When directing a mirror towards a neighbor, the mirror needs to be placed high enough to reflect their house. If it only reflects the fence separating your properties, the mirror cure will not be effective. Several of my clients have experienced great results from pointing a single mirror in the direction of a harmful neighbor's house. Often the neighbors find new homes out of the area and peace returns to the neighborhood.

Even when you have several difficult neighbors, it is unwise to use more than *ba–gua* mirror cure and it is certainly not a good idea to have four of them pointing in four different directions. Too much protection will block even good opportunities from coming to you; it will be as if you are living in a fortress. Although it may sound safe to be living within a stronghold, you will be isolated and therefore vulnerable because even though nothing can get in to hurt you, nothing can get in to help you either.

If you have a home business, it is best to completely avoid using a *ba–gua* mirror. You work hard to attract customers and clients, and your business needs to be open to all potential opportunities (while reserving the right not to do business with any of them for any reason). You are in business to solve the customers' and clients' problems. So, if you are trying to attract people with problems that your business aims to solve, placing a *ba–gua* mirror will put a boundary between you and future business. In effect, it could chase away future business.

If the traditional *ba–gua* mirror is not to your taste or does not fit with your overall décor, attractive alternatives are available in stained glass; but the most effective mirror for protection is the traditional design. There are a few additional styles of the classic *ba–gua* protection mirror, one of which is rectangular and has not only the eight trigrams but also a picture of the warrior God, (Guan Yu) riding a foo dog (*see* Animal Symbols, pp. 170). This mirror is most often used for aggressive protection when you are truly feeling unsafe in your own home.

If your *ba–gua* mirror falls, once in place, the security of the house has been compromised. Even if the cat knocks it over or some well–intentioned relative removes it, the meaning is the same: you should take precautions to protect the house.

Example: I remember years ago consulting on an older lady's apartment in a more dilapidated district outside of Los Angeles. She had decided to tape the *ba–gua* mirror onto the glass of her front window. She used strapping tape, the kind used on packages, and the kind that stays in place forever. Well, one day she called and said that the mirror fell and broke. I told her this was a bad sign, but she said, "No matter, I will be moving in a few weeks." I recommended that she move sooner and thankfully she did. A week later the apartment caught on fire and a great deal of damage was done to the building. If you place a *ba–gua* mirror and it falls, this is not a good sign. Consider clearing (*see* Clearing, pp. 133), and/or hanging or placing additional protection cures (though not more mirrors) and if you are getting ready to move, then just move!

Concave/Convex Mirrors

In addition to flat, ordinary mirrors and the special *ba–gua* mirror, there are two other mirrors commonly used in Feng Shui. One is concave, like the inside of a spoon. This mirror is hung to collect *Qi*. It is usually octagon–shaped and decorated with the eight trigrams and other Feng Shui symbols (perhaps Chinese representations of the constellations). This concave mirror is primarily used in cul–de–sacs or dead–end streets to help *Qi* pool. It is hung outside the home, facing the street, either from the house itself or a tree in the yard. The mirror gathers *Qi* energy to the house from the street, very much the way a lake gathers water from a stream. This *Qi* helps the family living in the house prosper.

A "cousin" to the concave mirror is the convex mirror (see fig. 29). This mirror is like the back of a spoon and it is used for an entirely different purpose. A convex mirror cure very aggressively sends Qi and, when pointed at a neighbor, can cause them to move. When applied, the force of this cure can be likened to giving people a large taste of their own medicine—whatever energy they send

Uses Of Mirrors

Fig. 31: A mirror can be used to bounce energy to a desired location. Here the street in front of the house represents the river of *Qi*. A small mirror placed on a tree can be positioned to bounce the energy from the street to the front door, bringing *Qi* into the house.

Fig. 32: To use the traditional or plain *ba–gua* mirror for protection place the mirror in the window nearest the front door. Place it inside the house facing out. The mirror can be set on the window sill or hung in the window. If there is no window by the front door then place the protection mirror in a bedroom window.

your way they are going to get back in return, with interest. Convex mirrors should be used sparingly and only when all other means have failed. Hang them so that they are high enough to clear fences and walls and reflect a view of the offending house. When the neighboring house is vacant, remove the mirror cure to allow new people to move in.

Uses of Mirrors

Mirrors are placed for six basic purposes and for each purpose, precise placement is important. Think of Qi as a ball on a pool table and the mirror as one of the side cushions. Set the mirror so that the energy will "bounce off" in the direction you would want it to go—as a ball would bounce off a pool table cushion on its way to sinking into the pocket. Keep in mind that line of sight is important. A billiard ball will not go into the pocket if an obstacle blocks the way. Qi, sent by the mirror, cannot hit your target if there is a physical object in the way.

Drawing Qi into the home: One use of a mirror is to draw Qi into a house from the outside. If the Qi within the house is too slow, and you are lacking the drive or the resources to get what you want, more Qi is needed. An abundance of Qi exists in the world. In the past (before an extensive road system), living, moving Qi meant an actual stream or river that went by your house. Where rivers represented the flow of Qi in the past, now *roads* bring the new Qi—especially the road that runs by your home. (If you live off the beaten path refer to Chapter 3, pp. 39 for suggestions on helping Qi find your dwelling.) Now, we want to direct the flow of Qi to your property.

Tip: Place a small mirror (between one and four inches in diameter), on a tree, a post, a pole, or on your mailbox so it reflects the street (see fig. 33). Place it in such a way that it can "bounce" the Qi from the street onto your front porch—the same way a pool player would bounce a ball—at an angle—off the pool–table cushion. The mirror can be attached with double–sided tape or Velcro. You may find you need more than one mirror to encourage the Qi to bounce all the way to your front door. This cure is especially helpful in those rare situations where your house sits behind another house. It is very hard for Qi to find your front door when a whole house divides you and the Qi flowing on the main street. In fact, without the mirrors to guide the *Qi*, the front house will absorb all of the *Qi* otherwise available to both houses. This could not only cause very low energy levels for the inhabitants of the house in back, it can also make it very difficult for them to move or to sell the house.

Tip: When using mirrors to direct *Qi* along a very long driveway, use safety mirrors. These mirrors are designed to help a driver navigate a hidden driveway or to see on–coming traffic. They also help to move *Qi*.

The Negative Wall: A mirror can be used to draw a person away from a *negative wall*. Negative walls can change positive energy into *sha Qi*. One example of a negative wall is any wall connecting your home with that of a difficult neighbor. If you live in a condominium, townhouse or apartment, you are likely to share walls with another unit. If you share such a wall with difficult neighbors, and do not want their troublesome *Qi* to seep over into your own home and affect your luck, use the cure described below.

Negative walls are not always walls shared with a neighbor, there can be negative walls inside your home. Any wall that has a commode on it is considered negative. If that wall is also a bedroom wall or kitchen wall it can bring negativity into that room. Most people are not sensitive to or affected by this wall, but when someone in the family is recovering from an illness or is susceptible to health concerns and sleeps in a room with such a wall, it is important to pull that individual's energy away from the wall itself.

Another instance of a negative wall is when a home shares a common wall with a trash collection area. This is commonly found in apartment complexes and condominiums where a common wall connects the apartment and the trash room.

Tip: The mirror cure can be small or large, decorative or plain. If the mirror(s) used for the cure is more than ten inches in diameter, be sure to follow the basic mirror placement rules previously described. To pull *Qi* away from a negative wall, place the mirror on the wall opposite to the problem wall.

Unhealthy shaped rooms: A few room shapes also contain walls that are considered "unhealthy," no matter what is on the other side of the wall. I refer specifically to the L–shaped "boot" and "knife" rooms. In boot–shaped rooms, one part of the "L" is much shorter than the other (see fig. 32). The far corner of the larger part of the "L" is the toe of the boot, and these walls are considered unlucky. When you sleep, work or try to relax in this area, you begin to feel that you are being stepped on, kicked around and/or squashed by life. This type of room creates too much pressure to live with.

In *knife–shaped rooms*, one part of the "L" is much narrower than the other, this is the handle of the knife and the wider leg of the "L," the chopping blade (see fig. 31). The blade wall is considered unlucky. Sleeping, working and relaxing on a blade is neither comfortable nor physically or mentally healthy.

Tip: The mirror cure can be small or large, decorative or plain. If the mirrors used for the cure are more than ten inches in diameter, be sure to follow the basic mirror placement rules previously discussed on pp. 149. To pull *Qi* away from a negative wall, place the mirror on the wall opposite to the problem wall. For example, if your sofa is on the blade of the knife and you don't want to move it, place a mirror directly opposite the sofa to draw energy away from that negative wall. However, do not place a mirror directly opposite a bed, it is considered bad luck. If you are sleeping on a negative wall, place a mirror on the opposite wall where it is not directly in line with the bed.

Reflect or Deflect Negative Energy: Sometimes we are so bombarded by stress in our daily lives that we become very sensitive to even slight points of stress. In these cases even something minor like sitting with your back to a door can start to manifest as neck pain, upper back problems, tightness in the chest, difficulty breathing or even low–grade depression. Our ancestors knew better than to relax with their backs to the cave entrance because they never knew when a hungry saber–toothed tiger would be walking by. Perhaps now we don't have wild animals creeping up behind us but we do have deadlines, obligations, and schedules and so in an effort not to cause ourselves additional stress it is important to reflect or deflect negative energy.

Tip: If you must sit with your back to the door, try placing a mirror in front of you at an angle so that you can see behind you while you are working, sitting or relaxing (see fig. 36). You will find that the mirror brings some peace of mind and allows you space to breathe. The mirror in this case can be large or small,

More Uses of Mirrors

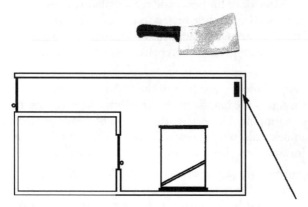

Fig. 33: The knife room is a room shaped like a cleaver. It is considered dangerous to sleep on the blade of the knife (shown by the bed position here), for the person will feel "on edge." If there is no alternative for the bed placement, then hang a mirror as shown to help neutralize the negative energy of the blade.

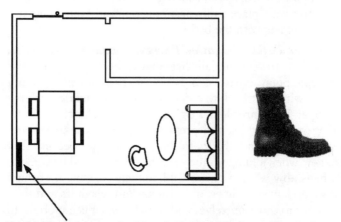

Fig. 34: The boot room is more of an even "L" shape. The most dangerous place to sit in a boot room is at the toe, (shown by the sofa position here) for a person sitting there will feel "stepped on." Ideally the sofa would be moved but if this is not practical then use a mirror as the cure. Placing a mirror opposite the seating area will help neutralize the negative energy of the boot.

decorative or plain. The position is what's important. You need to be able to see behind you while sitting, without having the mirror reflect something you do not want reflected. (The mirror should not reflect anything that you would not want to see more of—such as a toilet, an inbox or a pile of clutter.)

Close Walls: Close walls can be very oppressive. Many houses have a small entryway just inside the front door. This entryway is to allow for a transition from the outside world to the inside. However, in some cases there really isn't room for this entryway and we end up with a really closed–in space. If you walk into your home and are immediately faced with a wall, you feel blocked, and, in essence, the *Qi* is blocked also. All energy flow stops. You may have come home whistling a jaunty tune, thinking that you would have dinner ready in 15 minutes, feed the dog, throw in a load of laundry and start work on that novel you have been meaning to write but when you turn the key in the lock and open the door, you hit that wall and your energy simply drains away—all you can do is crawl to the sofa and hope that you know the pizza guy's phone number by heart. This is the kind of oppression people experience with a close wall.

Tip: The rule of thumb is that the height of the door is the minimum acceptable distance to the opposing wall. In other words, if the door were to fall inward and hit the opposite wall, the wall is too close. There are several cures for this outlined in the section on Entryways, pp. 53, but since many people like a mirror by the door so that they can check their appearance before leaving the house, let us discuss mirror placement. We do need a reflective surface to help the *Qi* that enters the house to disburse throughout the home, but we do not want the mirror to send the *Qi* back outside. Using our billiard ball analogy, we don't want to aim the ball directly at the opposing table cushion, as the ball will simply bounce right back at us. We want to hit the cushion at an angle. In this cure we want the mirror to be placed on a side wall. If the mirror can be placed so that it bounces *Qi* into a neighboring room (such as a main living area) all the better.

To Repel Evil: While we want to gather and bring in *Qi*, we want to reserve the right to refuse anyone or anything that may not have our best interests at heart. Here, the classic *ba–gua*

Still More Uses Of Mirrors

Fig. 35: In cases where the toilet can be seen from the kitchen, the front door or from bed you want to contain the negative energy of the bathroom. Place a small, plain mirror over the bathroom door facing into the bathroom (shown by small gray dot over door).

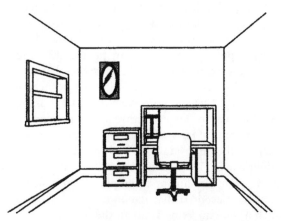

Fig. 36: When you are required to work sitting with your back to the door it is important to place a mirror on the wall or on your desk so you can see behind you. The mirror here is a symbol of protection and so whether you can see the door in it or not doesn't matter. It will bring better concentration and productivity.

protection mirror is needed in the front window. This mirror is described in more detail in the section, *Ba–gua* Mirrors, pp. 150.

The Commode: For providing us with an exceptionally useful mode of containing negative energy, we all owe a debt of gratitude to Mr. Crapper, the inventor of the flush toilet. His invention has made indoor bathrooms possible, and I have never met anyone who would give up this modern convenience for the sake of following traditional Feng Shui to the letter by placing all toilets outside the house. That thought in mind, a bathroom can contain noxious gasses and waste that we do not want to affect the *Qi* in the rest of the house. And, from a more aesthetic perspective, looking in from another room and seeing the toilet staring back at you is not a pleasant sight.

Tip: There are two instances when a mirror is employed to contain the *Qi* in a bathroom. The first is when the commode is visible from the front door. If the bathroom is (or can be) clearly seen from the entryway, the bathroom door should be closed (at least partially). In addition, a mirror should be hung over the door, facing into the bathroom (see fig. 35). This helps contain the negative toilet energy. The second instance concerns a private bathroom connected to a bedroom (often a master bedroom). When a person is lying in bed they should not be able to look over and see the toilet. Again, we are talking about seeing the actual bowl, not just a sink or bathtub. As in the first example, place a small mirror above the bathroom door, facing into the bathroom. It would also be helpful to keep the door closed if at all possible and to keep the toilet seat down.

In these instances the mirrors can be very small—even as small as one inch in diameter. They can be incorporated into a piece of art above the door. I have seen many creative solutions where miniature plaster angels, for instance, hold small mirrors or where a tiny mirror is the center of a silk flower arrangement. There are lovely, decorative mirrors in a variety of shapes and sizes, complete with carved wooden frames that might be suitable for this purpose as well.

Mirror Alternatives: In addition to mirrors, you might consider using pictures framed with glass in front. Pictures with dark backgrounds produce a very clear reflection. Computer monitors and television screens are also "mirrors" when dark. In the past, pots and pans have been used as mirrors and also other brass items. Sometimes knives can act as small mirrors (though these are considered very aggressive mirrors, and should be used carefully). Windows, however, are not considered mirrors, even when it is dark outside. This is because—in spite of being quite reflective—they are connectors between the inside and outside world and therefore hardly protective.

Broken Mirrors: Broken mirrors should never be used as Feng Shui cures. Besides bringing (according to tradition) the possibility of seven years' bad luck, they fracture the Qi, causing it to splinter and go off in various directions. Discard a mirror once it has been broken and remove the resulting *sha Qi* from your home.

Chapter 10

Sound Cures

Bells

A wide variety of bells are used in Feng Shui. There are both single bells and strings of bells. When choosing a bell (or bells) consider the material of which the bell is made, the design and the sound. The most common bells used in Feng Shui are brass bells (see fig. 37). These may be shiny or embossed with designs. Classic Chinese bells may have dragons, boats, religious figures and sayings carved on them. In keeping with the guidelines for using most traditional cures, you need only match the design on the bell to the type of *Qi* you are trying to attract in order to find them very effective. Here are some specific bell cures:

1. *Combat an interior poison arrow:* A poison arrow is a protruding corner that slices into the flow of *Qi* in a home, creating disruption; it commonly causes disharmony, argumentativeness and unhappiness for those who dwell in the house. (Note: Some exterior poison arrows can be cured using a mirror. Refer to the sections Exteriors, pp. 32, and Mirrors, pp. 147, for more information.) Poison arrows are often found in bedrooms, L-shaped living rooms and hallways. To deflect the energy slicing through the room, hang a bell in front of the arrow (see fig. 38). This neutralizes the negative energy and balances *Qi*.

2. *Bell strings* are the cure of choice for dealing with poison arrows because a string of bells covers more area than a single bell. If you are selecting a bell string, consider one that has brass bells and a pleasant sound. You may want to manually ring them every once in a while to maintain balanced and harmonious *Qi* in the area. Bell strings can be strung with string in a variety of colors. Any color that coordinates with your décor is suitable.

3. *Single bells* can be used to call or invite positive *Qi* to enter a home. They can sometimes be used in place of wind chimes. Place the bell in a window facing the street and ring it often to call new energy.

Bells and Bell Strings

Fig. 37: Traditional Feng Shui bells are usually made of metal and are embossed with pictures and Chinese characters. The bell shown here is shaped like a pagoda, a symbol of peace. It is topped with a knot, a graphic depiction of the word China in Chinese and attached to the clapper is a Chinese coin with it's distinctive square hole representing prosperity and abundance.

Fig. 38: Bells and bell strings are often used to combat internal poison arrows; a protruding corner that points to a sitting or sleeping area. A poison arrow can divide a family or create stress within a person so that one feels irritable, scattered and unappreciated. Hang the bell or bell string in front of the protruding corner to combat the energy of the poison arrow.

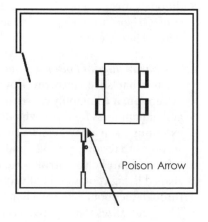

Poison Arrow

Single Bells are traditionally used for the combined purposes of calling energy and protecting the house. This type of use is necessary when the house sits at a T–intersection. The purpose is to protect the house from the direct line of traffic flow, while at the same time inviting positive energy to the house. A brass bell embossed with protective symbols such as dragons, religious figures or protective words and phrases will disburse the *sha Qi* and welcome positive *sheng Qi*.

4. *Use bells to call energy to a bedroom.* Because they can sound sweet, bells are specifically used to call love and romance to the bedroom. Simply hang a string of bells or a single bell in the bedroom near the bed (but out of the way of anyone getting in or out of bed. We don't want people hitting their heads on the bell). Remember to chime the bells whenever you are in the room.

5. *Use bells to clear and protect an area.* For as long as there have been shops and shopkeepers, bells have been hung on doors. This practice began not only as a way to alert the shopkeeper that a customer had arrived, but also to scare away any evil spirits the customer may have inadvertently brought into the space. You can protect your home with bells as well. Walk through your home loudly ringing a large, clear–sounding bell or a string of large bells, whichever you prefer. As you proceed you may want to say, "I command all evil to depart." or, "I demand that all negativity leave this place." Walk through the entire house, completing your process at the front door. Push the evil out of the house like you would an unwelcome guest. Then, put the bells away until you need them the next time. This cure is best performed a couple of times per year.

Flutes

The flute is a classic Feng Shui cure—a symbol of harmony in the house. We place flutes in homes where there is discord. It is said that arguing people expel a lot of "hot air." This air goes through the flute which transforms it to sweet, melodious sound. Flutes are often made of inexpensive bamboo, decorated with red cord or string. However, metal flutes are also a good choice. And

I have used some classic Native American–type flutes that have been very effective. Choose a flute that works with your décor.

Exposed beams can be very hard on Qi. The Qi bounces off the beams at weird angles. People living in such a house can become very unhappy as a result of this disruptive energy. They will argue, fight, manipulate, attempt to control, worse, scheme against each other. Hang flutes on one of the beams to help calm the Qi.

Tip: The flute cure consists of hanging flutes in pairs, customarily using red string to hold them in place. Some traditional Feng Shui flutes have red tassels, although this is not required. Hang the flutes with the mouthpiece facing down and into the space below. Only one pair of flutes is necessary per room. If you cannot bring yourself to put the flutes on the beam itself, or if you feel it conflicts with the overall décor of the room, then hang them on a wall or place them on a shelf. Even this will bring some relief to the unrest in the house.

Wind Chimes

Wind Chimes are a popular cure in Feng Shui. They can be used inside or out. They come in many styles, so blending with any décor is easy. Since each type of wind chime has a specific use and energy, it is important that the design you choose be in harmony with what you want to attract. There are too many types of wind chimes to describe them all here, but we will review a few to get you started.

Celestial objects such as the sun, moon and stars bring an energy of help and assistance from above. The sun brings help with confidence and personal power. The sun's image will help you shine as you move along the pathways towards your goals, and it will light your path when you are unsure how to proceed. The moon will bring you what you need to feel emotionally fulfilled—a sense of being nurtured and cared for. Moon Qi is like that of a loving mother, gently watching over you at home. The stars bring us guidance from a heavenly source. Stars, like angels, guard us from danger, keep us company in lonely times and hold our hands when we meet life's challenges.

A **single bird** is the symbol of freedom. This symbol suggests the ability to soar above the mundane aspects of living as we seek to experience life in an extraordinary way. Chimes with bird symbolism call all feathered creatures to aid us as we travel; they allow us to rise above the practical problems of our everyday lives and project ourselves into the future as they protect us from anything (or anyone) who might prevent us from doing and being our best.

Flowers bring joy, a joy often felt when needs and desires are met, when there is no fear of the future and no chains tying us to the past. Flowers symbolize companionship, from friendship to passionate love. Flowers bring variety to our daily lives.

Wind chimes decorated with specific **animal representations** bring different *Qi* based on the animal's primary attributes. A good rule of thumb is that if you are attracted to the animal, you probably need the specific *Qi* in your life at this time. On the whole, animals represent unconditional love. Animal chimes work very well at attracting more love into your life. They help enhance feelings of self–love and self–acceptance. Animals also represent their specific animal abilities. Using cures that incorporate animal representations, we can experience the agility of the cat, the loyalty of the dog, the gentleness of the deer and more.

In Feng Shui, **fish** represent money. Hanging fish wind chimes attracts money *Qi* into your house. Sometimes this will bring more work or a better job, sometimes an opportunity or an unexpected windfall.

The materials that make up the wind chime also affect the type of *Qi* the chime calls. Here is a short list of common wind chime materials and finishes:

Gold–toned wind chimes energize your own innate talents. They promote success, courage and confidence. If you need extra willpower, a golden–toned chime is a good choice. The gold tone also attracts financial benefit. Chimes of this color help grown children living in the home to feel a burst of independence, the desire to get out and find their first job in order to create the beginnings of their own financial stability.

Silver–toned wind chimes bring better family communication and a stable, regular income. If the people living in the house are angry or argumentative with one another, silver–colored chimes are the optimal cure. When one of the residents fears a layoff or is facing other types of job uncertainty, a silver–tone chime calls new career opportunities.

Brass is a popular metal often used in the manufacture of wind chimes. Brass chimes attract career opportunities and help maintain good reputations for all living in the space. If you have your own business or are looking to move up in your place of employment, a brass wind chime calls lucky *Qi* to encourage and implement expansion and promotion. This type of wind chime will also bring you recognition for both career and personal achievements of all kinds. In addition, it brings favorable notice from family members for the work that's done at home.

Copper is a warm, beautiful metal. Used in a wind chime, it calls healing energy into the household. For centuries this metal has been worn by people experiencing health problems for healing and helping them toward wellness. Copper also attracts love and friendship. Historically this metal has been associated with the planet, Venus, the planet of love. Place a copper wind chime outside your home and its sound will call love into your life.

Iron is a strong, heavy, dark metal—unfortunately rarely used for wind chimes. Iron wind chimes guard the house and protect it from physical and spiritual threats. Iron can help protect your finances from the ups and downs of a fickle economy; it can also protect the health and well–being of those who live inside. Too much iron (as in iron bars over windows or doors) can feel like a prison to those inside. If you already have ironwork or iron bars as exterior (or interior) design elements, do not add an iron wind chime.

Steel is a newer metal, strong and shiny. It promotes healthful, restful sleep. If you wake frequently at night or have trouble falling asleep, the gentle sound of steel wind chimes can help. Steel also guards you from nightmares and other negative thoughts that may come at night. If children are afraid of the dark, steel wind chimes can soothe their fears and help them to drift peacefully into slumber.

Patina is a thin, moss–green layer that forms on copper or bronze. Lately this has become a very popular look for wind chimes and other outdoor decorative items. Patina attracts *Qi* to heal past wounds and painful childhood issues. Many struggle with challenges arising from their childhood or upbringing. Hanging this type of wind chime calls the kind of *Qi* that will lessen the pain of the past, create a safe environment where childhood traumas can be eased, allowing people to move forward, unshackled from painful memories.

Clay is used to make beautiful wind chimes that resonate with a pleasant, natural sound. Clay is of the earth and so attracts material things into the home. If you are just starting out in life, building your first home or if you need many things in order to make your house a home, a clay wind chime is a great choice. Clay also brings fertility Qi to those trying to conceive. It is said that the gentle sounds of a clay wind chime call little souls to come to you.

Here are some rules for hanging wind chimes:

1 Hang the chime high enough so that it doesn't obstruct a path; the tallest member of the household should be able to walk under a chime without bumping into it.

2 Hang this cure in a place where it will not chime incessantly. Shelter your chime from constant wind, making sure that there are periods when the chime rings and periods when it is quiet. Constant chiming is simply irritating.

3 If the chime is hung in a place where it never feels the breath of the wind, chime it manually. Sometimes we hang chimes indoors or on enclosed porches where the wind will never reach them. It is then up to you to call Qi by manually ringing the chime a few times a week.

4 Hang a chime so that it rings when a door is opened. Tradition says that this will both call new Qi and frighten away any evil spirits lurking in the vicinity.

5 Every few months dust off the wind chime, polish the rods and remove any cobwebs that may have attached themselves to it. This will reactivate the chime cure, making it strong again.

Chapter 11

Living Cures

Animal Symbols

Animal symbols are important Feng Shui cures. They can be used to quickly alter the quality of Qi in a space. Because the world is filled with animal lovers, you may already have many wonderful animal symbols in your house. It is good to know what these symbols mean to make sure you are attracting the type of Qi you want in your home. Even though it is generally easy to read the significance of animal symbols, we need to recognize that different cultures have created a variety of myths about animals. Sometimes an animal that is revered in one part of the world is despised in another.

Let us for a moment consider the symbolism of the rat. In this country a clear image comes to mind—usually unpleasant. In China, however, the rat is the first symbol of the Chinese Zodiac, as the following story explains. Buddha lay dying; knowing that death was imminent, he called the animals to his side. The cat was among those called but was napping. The rat, seeing this, raced past the soundly sleeping cat and arrived at Buddha's side first. Because of his prompt response to the call and intrinsic industry the rat was pronounced "first" in the procession of the Chinese Zodiac.

Those of us in the West, born in the Chinese Year of the Rat, may consider what we know (from a cultural and societal perspective) about rats and feel this is no compliment. (Rats do not have a respected reputation here in the U.S.) But we have our own mythology surrounding a relative of this powerful Chinese symbol. Think for a moment of the mouse—like Mickey and that pint–size guy, Stuart Little, and realize that a part of our psyche accepts this creature as "cute," honorable and hard–working. However, because of the way most of us view rats in this country and in our culture, it would probably be best not to decorate a house in a rat motif. (But, if you have a special affection for Mickey or Stuart Little, and wanted to celebrate the qualities of the Chinese Rat, a cute mouse or two would be fine.)

To effectively use an animal symbol as a cure, you need to find an animal you like whose main qualities are in harmony with the quality of *Qi* you are trying to attract. For instance, you may love eagles, but if you are seeking to become a champion swimmer this is not a good animal symbol for you because eagles are not great swimmers. Or, you may know that in Asia bats are regarded as a symbol of prosperity but if the thought of a bat makes you want to run screaming out of the room, don't decorate with bats. Why? Because blind panic does not attract prosperity.

Placing your animal symbol cure. Once you have identified the animal symbol that harmonizes with the type of *Qi* you want to attract into your life, you will need to find a good representation of that animal. Animal symbols can be art, statues, stuffed animals, figurines, plaques, wood carvings, etc. The depiction can either be realistic or stylized. The most important thing is to choose a style that fits with your overall décor.

Generally speaking, animal symbols should be placed in the area of the house associated with the *Qi* represented by the animal; symbols for romance go in the bedroom, symbols for money go in the home office, symbols for health go in the kitchen, symbols for protection go near the front door, etc. When placing your animal cure, take care to find a special spot. It has a special job, so give it a special place from which to do that job.

Let us discuss the energy represented by some animals and insects and determine how we can best use these symbols in the home.

Ant: Though I have yet to see a home decorated with ants (infested perhaps, but never decorated), they are considered a very honorable insect in Chinese tradition. They represent virtue, patriotism and the gain that results from hard work. On the other hand, ants can also represent self–interest. This quality is not considered favorable in a community–oriented society like China, but here in the independent West, it may not be such a bad thing. If you do decide to decorate with ants, they are most effectively displayed in the home office. If ants decide to come in and "decorate" (or infest) your house, it means that lots of work is coming your way.

Bat: Bats are looked upon very favorably in the East, since the Chinese word for "bat" and the one for "happiness" are homonyms. Bats are used extensively in artwork and decoration in China and are symbols of joy and longevity. If you like bats (They are helpful, eating their full body weight in flying insects nightly. This means that in North America alone, millions of pounds of crop–consuming pests become "dinner" every night), then you can use them in your décor. However, if you associate bats with blood–drinking, black–wearing, coffin–dwelling vampires, then a bat motif will attract a very different energy. The best location for a bat cure would be in the living room, family room or bathroom.

Bear: Several varieties of bears and bear–like animals lived and live in China, among them the black bear and the panda. Bears are a symbol of bravery and strength. They are thought to be a powerful protection against robbers. Bear symbols can be placed in the home office, bedroom (see note on teddy bears below), living room or kitchen.

Bear, Teddy: We need to talk about your teddy bear collection. The symbol of a teddy bear is different than that of a real bear. Teddy bears bring comfort to those who have to sleep alone. This is not a conducive cure to use to attract a new relationship. This classic toy, once reserved for children, has gained so much popularity these days it is rare that I find a house without at least one bear displayed (some families have dozens). Teddy bears are fine . . .unless you are actively looking for love. If you want love in your life and love in your bed, you must make room for it. Ditch the bear(s) until Prince (or Princess) Charming makes their appearance. Put teddy in a box or in a closet and allow love a little room in your bed. Once you are in a happy relationship, teddy can come back out to play.

Bee: Bees give us sweet honey but have that sharp stinger as well—kind of a mixed bag. The bee is a symbol of industry and thrift, two prized attributes in Chinese culture. Bees are also perceived to work well with others being both community–minded and sociable. Place bee symbols in the living room or outside on the porch. Because of the stinger, don't place bee symbols in children's rooms. If you are allergic to bee stings, don't use this symbol as a cure. No sense in attracting something that can kill you.

Butterfly: In China there are many, many varieties of butterflies. They are prevalent in artwork and poetry. Butterflies are a symbol of happy married life. The butterfly symbol can be used in the bedroom, living room or in front of the house to attract love and a happy marriage.

Cat: Since the cat is not a member of the Chinese Zodiac, it is thought that cats are not indigenous to China—even though they are mentioned in texts predating Christianity. Cat symbols (and actual cats living in your home) represent protection. In China, cats are prized for protecting silkworms (silkworms are eaten by rats, which are then eaten by cats). The Chinese say that cats can fight evil spirits and protect the house. It is also said that if a strange cat comes to your door, you need its protection because some hidden evil is robbing you of your wealth. Cats teach us about emotionally healthy relationships—both how to love and how to let go. Since it is impossible to tell a cat where he or she should be, cats are usually allowed to go anywhere in the house. For that reason cat symbol cures can be placed in any room.

Cat, Lucky: A Lucky cat or "beckoning cat" is a small statue of a cat, sitting up on his haunches and waving. He is usually holding a little sign that, loosely translated, says "100 million pounds of gold." He waves his paw in order to attract money. This cure usually comes in the form of a coin bank and is placed in the window or in view of the door in homes and businesses to call money. It is said that if a coin is fed to the lucky cat each week, he will bring good fortune and money to all who dwell in his house. This cure comes in gold (to attract large sums of money), white (for good health) and black (for prosperous business).

Crane: In Chinese lore, the crane's abilities are almost legendary. It has been said they can live 600 years, live without food, and change into human form. It is also said that some people (after having lived to a very old age) would turn themselves into cranes and fly to heaven. Cranes are a symbol of longevity and can be used as cures in the bedroom, living room or kitchen.

Cricket: Crickets are symbols of luck and courage. It is unlucky to kill a cricket that enters your house. Place cricket symbols in the living room or children's rooms.

Deer: Deer are another longevity symbol and are reputed to be the only animal that found the sacred fungus of immortality (mushrooms). Deer also give us an awareness of danger which enables us to get out of harm's way. Deer can be placed near the front door, in the kitchen or in bedrooms.

Dog: Despite the fact that this creature has been considered a delicacy in Chinese cuisine, dogs are also pets—loved and cared for in much the same way as we love and care for our pets here in the West. In fact, some of the ancient Chinese emperors were known to bestow rank on their dogs. When a strange dog arrives at your door, it means money is coming. In general, dog symbols represent courage, loyalty and fidelity. Dog symbols can be placed in the bedroom, living room or home office.

Dogs, Foo: (fu dogs) Foo dogs are powerful protection symbols. These statues are always displayed in pairs and are usually found flanking a door. The one with his foot on the world is the male, the female has her foot on the baby (in a protective sense, not a squish–the–baby sense). They are placed so that their raised paws are closest to each other. Place your foo dogs on either side of your front door or in a window in the living room.

Dove: Doves are a symbol of long life, faithfulness and filial duty. They can be placed in the bedroom or living room.

Dragon: The dragon is very special to the Chinese. It is considered to be an animal of great wisdom, longevity and power. It is the only mythical creature in the Chinese Zodiac, suggesting that at one time dragons really did exist. Books written as far back as 200 C.E. mention the dragon in the accounting of species of fish, snakes and lizards. The azure dragon is one of the four supernatural animals that guard the cardinal directions. The azure dragon guards the east, the others are the white tiger (west), the black tortoise (north), and the red phoenix (south).

Some say that there are three types of dragons. The most powerful of them, *Long,* the "wind dragon," lives in the sky. *Li,* the "water dragon," lives in the ocean. *Jiao,* the "earth dragon," lives on land, in the mountains and marshes. As the wind dragon meets the water dragon, clouds form and rain falls. The rain helps shape the landscape, forming mountain ranges and vast plains. These mountain ranges are the earth dragons and stand tall, holding the wind and allowing clouds to form and *Qi* to accumulate. This interactive cycle of the three dragons shows that the Chinese were aware of the concepts of evaporation and cloud formation long before we in the West understood this natural process.

At the top of each mountain live the "dragon kings." These are mediators between heaven and earth. They watch and regulate the cycle of the three dragons. They control the weather by regulating the five weather elements: rain, sunshine, heat, cold and wind. Of these, only wind (*feng*) and rain (*shui*) can move. This is why we use Feng Shui to attempt to balance these two particular forces and achieve harmony in our environment.

Other ancient Chinese authors talk about different dragons. The *Celestial Dragon* lives in the sky and protects heaven. The *Spiritual Dragon* flies, producing wind and rain. The *Dragon of the Hidden Treasures* guards the wealth that is concealed from the eyes of man. And there are the *Winged Dragon*, the *Horned Dragon*, the *Coiled Dragon* and the *Yellow Dragon* whose purposes and powers are more obscure.

There are nine dragons depicted in art and carvings. *Pu lao*, one that can sing, is carved onto bells. *Qiu Niu* loves music, so is found on musical instruments. *Pi shi* loves literature and is found on stone tablets. *Ba Xia* has strength enough to support great weight and so is carved into stone at the base of buildings. *Chao feng* loves danger and is carved into the eaves of temples. *Chi wen* loves the water and so was carved on the beams on bridges. *Suan ni* honors rest and relaxation and is found on thrones and temple chairs. *Ya zu* excels at war and is found on the hilts of weapons. And finally, *Bi an*, a master of litigation, is carved on prison gates.

Dragons are often depicted holding or standing on a ball. This ball represents the "pearl of potentiality" also known as the *Cosmic Egg*. Sometimes dragons are shown in pairs, fighting for the pearl. The story comes down from the Ching Dynasty where it was said that a minister of state found a wounded snake; he gave the snake medicine and the snake was healed. One day the snake returned to the minister and said he was the son of a dragon. He offered the minister this valuable pearl as thanks for saving his life. Since then, the dragon has been depicted with the pearl.

The symbol of the dragon represents strength, health and the strongest of positive magic. Place a picture or statue of a dragon near the front door, facing out. You can also place dragons in the living room, kitchen or family room. This will help protect the family's health and well–being.

Dragon–headed Turtle: This special symbol combines the power of the dragon with the long life of the turtle and is used especially to protect the wealth and health of the head of the household. It is also said that if you tie a ribbon of red or blue around the mouth of the beast, arguing will cease in the home.

Dragonfly: A symbol of wind and summer; a symbol that reminds us that sometimes small, gentle things can have big, scary names. It reminds us that even though a task or goal may sound daunting, even overwhelming, it may be simple and easy. Dragonflies can be placed in home offices, family rooms and dining rooms.

Duck: Ducks are a symbol of felicity and joy. The mandarin duck, a particularly beautiful bird, has a unique quality in that it becomes singularly attached to its mate. If separated, it will pine away and die. For this reason, pairs of mandarin ducks symbolize happy marriage and conjugal fidelity. Ducks can be placed in the family room and mandarin ducks in the bedroom.

Elephant: A symbol of great strength, the elephant is also a symbol of wealth, power and prudence. Elephants should be placed in the living room, near the entryway or in the home office. They should face the door, and are best depicted with the end of their trunks pointing up.

Falcon: Falcons and other birds of prey symbolize keen eyesight, bold moves and military skill. They can be placed in the home office.

Fish: For centuries fish have been a major part of the Chinese diet. Fish are indisputably important to the survival and prosperity of the people of China. The word for fish (*yu*) sounds like the Chinese word for surplus (*yu*). This link between the two words strengthens the traditional concept that fish symbolize wealth and prosperity. Fish symbols are usually placed by the front door, in the home office or the kitchen.

Fish, Double: Two fish hung together, usually with a coin, are a symbol of the old Chinese saying, "May you have left–over money every year." Double fish can be hung in the kitchen, home office, or by the front door to welcome extra money into the house.

Animal Cures

Lucky Cat, whose sign loosely translates as "100 million pounds of gold", is said to call wealth with his raised paw.

Bats are popular because the Chinese words for bat and happiness are homonyms, making this animal lucky.

The great Foo Dogs guard many temples and businesses. They are a symbol of valor, loyalty and energy.

The Dragon is the most powerful animal of Chinese lore, and the only mythical animal of the Chinese Zodiac. It is said to protect ones health and bring ultimate power.

The Lucky Money Frog is a three legged frog who has a coin in his mouth. He is placed near the entrance to the home facing the door ready to welcome guests... and welcome money.

Fox: In Chinese lore the fox is seen as unlucky, because they were often found around graves. Foxes are said to ferry souls to the land of the dead. It is best not to decorate with a fox motif.

Frog: The frog or toad, specifically the three–legged variety, is said to attract wealth. This creature is usually depicted sitting on a pile of coins, with one in his mouth. The representation is placed by the front door, facing outside, and is said to attract wealth to the house. If you don't have three–legged frogs, the four–legged ones will do.

Goose: Like ducks, geese are symbols of happy marriages. It is said that a goose never takes a second mate and so the goose is a symbol used to honor the memory of a spouse who has passed away. If you have already been married and you want to attract another mate, a couple of ducks would make a better cure than a gaggle of geese.

Horse: Horses came early to China via central Asia and were honored for their speed, beauty and grace. Horses symbolize quickness—both in mind and in action—and they represent the heart of perseverance. Horses can be placed in any room of the house.

Lion: Lions are not indigenous to China and are therefore not seen in ancient texts or primitive artworks. However, they are important symbols in Feng Shui. Sometimes the foo dogs are called "foo lions" (*see* Dog) and are placed to guard buildings. Lions are a symbol of valor, energy and the wisdom to rule. The "Dance of the Lion," where men put on a large paper lion and dance through the streets, is part of the Festival of Lanterns celebrated on the fifteenth day of the first lunar month. Lion symbols can be placed in any room; they should face the door.

Monkey: Monkeys are a symbol of cleverness and success. They chase away evil spirits and are believed to bestow health and well–being on mankind. Monkey depictions can be displayed in the living room or family room. Due to the monkey's tendencies for trickery, it is not recommended that monkeys be in the bedroom or home office.

Ox: Oxen or cows are a symbol of springtime, of hard work, industry and rewards that come as a result of thrift. I have seen many a kitchen decorated with the cow motif and I have met the hard–working people who cook and eat in those kitchens. Ox and cow symbols should be used sparingly and are most commonly displayed in the kitchen or dining room.

Parrot: Parrots are a warning that one should be faithful to one's spouse. There is an old saying, "don't tell your secrets to a parrot," meaning that if you tell your plans to one person, you might as well tell the world. However, if you think your spouse is hiding something from you, a parrot picture might be a good addition to the bedroom.

Peacock: Male peacocks are a symbol of beauty and dignity. They can be placed in the bedroom or living room. The feathers are said to attract marriage proposals.

Phoenix: The phoenix, guarding south, is one of the four creatures that watch over the four points of the compass (along with the dragon, tiger and tortoise). It was said to live for 500 years and then consume itself in flames; later, a new phoenix would rise out of the ashes. The Chinese have written accounts of this bird dating back to 2600 B.C.E. The phoenix is often paired with the dragon in artwork and carvings as a symbol of a balance of power. The phoenix is a symbol of peace and prosperity and can be placed in any room except a child's room.

Pig: Also known as "the long–nosed general," the pig is an honorable animal in Chinese lore. In fact, the Chinese character for *home* is the ideogram for pig–under–a–roof. Pigs are symbols of rest, relaxation and serenity. Best not to place them in areas where you want to stay busy.

Rabbit: Rabbits or hares are plentiful in China. They are a symbol of longevity and fertility. White rabbits mean a long and fruitful life, red rabbits mean very good luck. If you don't want pregnancy, keep bunnies out of the bedroom.

Ram: Rams, sheep and goats are symbols of retirement and a peaceful life. The lamb is a symbol of respect because it kneels before its mother to take milk. It is generally not a good idea to place a lamb symbol in your office or business, because you may end up pleading with all your customers. Rams, sheep and goats may be placed in a living room or a family room to promote tranquility.

Rat: Though in the West we are not thrilled with the image of the rat (unless his first name is Mickey), the Chinese see them as a noble animal, industrious and thrifty. Though rats bring luck, if you don't think they are cute, you probably should select some other symbol or cure to represent this *Qi* such as the ox.

Snake: Since the beginning of time an uneasy relationship has existed between people and snakes. The snake both inspires awe and represents treachery, it is serene, cool, collected and observant. In order to successfully display snake symbols, it is important that you really like snakes. A snake can most successfully be displayed in the home office or in the kitchen. Snakes should not be placed in the bedroom—in case that treacherous side raises its head.

Spider: There are two basic types of spiders, one the brown, friendly, *Charlotte's Web* type and the other, the poisonous black widow type. Friendly spiders symbolize building and creating something intricate. Black widows are a symbol of danger and dark power. Use spider symbols sparingly and not in children's rooms.

Tiger: Tigers were at one time plentiful in China. They are considered the king of all forest animals. The tiger symbol is one that represents political power, dignity and courage. Tigers should face the doorway, ready to "eat" any evil–intentioned person who might approach. They can be placed in the home office, kitchen or at the end of hallways. They can also be placed to combat the mouth–of–the–dragon energy found in rooms at the end of long hallways. Place the tiger in this room to balance the excessive dragon energy.

Tortoise: One of the four creatures guarding the four directions, the tortoise (guarding north) is said to live for thousands of years. It is a symbol of longevity and endurance. There are many legends about the tortoise and his shell. A monk once found a tortoise whose shell had special markings, and from these he derived the *I Ching,* a famed oracle still used today. Turtles and tortoises can be used in bedrooms, living rooms and entryways.

Unicorn: Perhaps unicorns once roamed the land in China— their memory still survives, mentioned in both ancient and modern texts and portrayed in many art forms. The unicorn is a symbol of happiness, purity and grandeur. This creature was endowed with many powers, including an ability to walk on water. It was believed to display benevolence toward all other life forms. It was a horse–like animal, the male with a single horn, the female, hornless. It was said to be red, yellow, blue, white and black, with yellow under the belly. Its voice was likened to a bell. You can place unicorn symbols in living rooms, dining rooms and family rooms.

Wasp: Unlike bees, wasps are nasty tempered, well–armed flying insects that do not give us honey. Wasps bring bad luck with neighbors (a sign they will spread gossip about you in the community). Remove wasps' nests as soon as safely possible.

Wolf: Wolves are a symbol of independence and cunning. Wolves are sometimes symbolized as taking advantage of the weak or defenseless. Use the wolf representation sparingly.

Indoor Plants

Plants are considered wonderful and useful Feng Shui cures. Healthy plants can aid in supporting your own health and well–being. They contribute not only their beauty but also oxygen to any environment. They bring with them lucky *Qi* that promotes positive, healthful energy.

If you have no talent for keeping plants alive, silk plants are a good compromise. Find high quality silk plants that look as real as possible. On the other hand, plastic plants—especially ones that look plastic—will not bring you or your home any benefit so you may as well toss them out.

Dried flowers and plants, while often attractive, bring a problem. Dried plants are literally dead plants, so they cannot bring any new *Qi* into your life. They will attract the *Qi* of the past. If you have a lot of dried flowers, you may be holding onto the past too tightly. And if you want to attract a new relationship, new job, new anything, dried plants will not attract the type of *Qi* you want. The rule is, one dried arrangement per room maximum, and better to have none.

Of course, there are a million varieties of plants and it is well beyond the scope of this book to list the meaning of each and every one. That said, know that each plant does have its own special energy and meaning. In general, it is relatively easy to choose the right plant to represent the type of *Qi* you want to attract. Be mindful when placing plants. Place them where they will flourish, where they will not block access to something you need and where they can be watered easily without damaging furniture or flooring.

Plants with rounded leaves: These bring wealth, money and ease. They are ideally placed in entryways (as long as they don't block the door), in living areas, home offices and bathrooms.

Plants with spikes, thorns and needles: These plants offer protection. They block *sha Qi* and protect you and your home (and your loved ones). They are well placed at bedroom windows (inside or out) to protect you from the outside world while you sleep. These are sometimes usefully placed on your desk at work when you are bothered by difficult circumstances or troublesome co-workers.

Flowering plants: These bring joy and brighten a person's life. They are nice in the living room, the bedroom, the kitchen and in children's rooms. I have heard some Feng Shui practitioners say a plant in the bedroom was bad for the health, as it would "steal your breath." This is not true. Plants do process what we exhale, but they convert it into health–giving oxygen. So, add plants to any room you like, and breathe deeply.

All other indoor plants: All of the other plants (those with no spikes, no round leaves and no flowers) still facilitate growth and healing, and create good *Qi* in the house. Put in as many plants as you can easily take care of. And, enjoy!

Outdoor Plants

Aloe: A healing plant, its leaves can be cut open and used to heal burns. This plant, because of its healing nature and spiky appearance, is a protective plant and can guard the house from evil.

Azalea: A beautiful but poisonous plant, in China the azalea is sometimes called "tiger flower." When it grows in your garden its benefits include sexual potency and beauty.

Bamboo: There are innumerable uses for bamboo in China. This plant is used for food, paper, pipes, buckets, furniture, roofs, packing material and medicines. Bamboo is often used in art to symbolize longevity, stability and love for family.

Cactus: This family of plants is considered unlucky for fertility. A strip of red paper is often hung from the cactus to protect the family from any evil spirits that might use the cactus thorns to hurt them.

Note: Having lived in the southwest United States for more than a decade, I have seen a lot of cacti. While all plants create and attract *Qi*—create because they are living things—cacti, with its sharp pointy ends, are the plants for protection. Too much protection will cut you off from the world, making it very difficult for *Qi* and opportunities to reach you. So, while a couple of cactus plants are OK (especially if you are living in a climate where cacti thrive), moderation is better. And a cactus should not be allowed to impede a path, block an entrance or be in direct line with an entryway. If placed under a bedroom window, the cactus will absolutely protect the person who sleeps inside, however, should there be an urgent need to get out using the window (say, in the instance of a fire), the cactus will prove not to be such a good idea. Use cacti sparingly.

Chrysanthemum: These lovely plants flourish in China and symbolize autumn. The ninth lunar month of the Chinese calendar is said to be the "chrysanthemum month" and during this month people make a point of going out to see the beautiful blossoms. This plant is a symbol of joviality, a life of pleasure and a happy retirement.

Forget–Me–Not: A native plant to Europe and the United States, forget–me–not blossoms help us remember. Grow this plant if you want to improve your memory.

Garlic: Native to Europe, garlic has been used for centuries to guard against evil. It is said to protect people from many things— everything from vampires to the plague. Grown in the garden it protects the house and brings flavor to life (and to our cuisine).

Ginseng: Ginseng is grown and consumed to ensure sexual potency.

Ivy: Growing around your property, ivy encourages fidelity and guards against disaster.

Jasmine: Originally brought to China from Persia, jasmine is used to scent tea and make oils. It is a symbol of the fair sex and of sweetness in life.

Plant Cures

Lucky bamboo,
very popualar now,
is an ancient cure
to promote virtue
and longevity.

The orchid is a symbol
of refined beauty,
fertility and success.

The peony, a symbol of good
fortune and feminine beauty,
is often used to attract love.

Cacti should be used sparingly
but when used is a great protection
cure. All the spiky varieties ward off
unwelcome visitors.

The jade plant (crassula argentea) is considered
lucky for being called jade, the honored stone in
Chinese lore, and because its round leaf is said to
attract money.

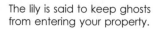

The lily is said to keep ghosts
from entering your property.

Lavender: This plant symbolizes cleanliness, peacefulness and tranquility.

Lilac: This plant should not be grown indoors because its name in Chinese sounds like the word for nail—sharp and pointed—and could cause family strife. But outdoors this plant is said to keep evil away and attract only good things.

Lily: Lilies are planted to dispel grief. It is also believed that lilies planted on your grounds can keep ghosts from entering your property.

Lotus: The lotus flower is sacred in China. Every part of this plant has a use. It is considered a symbol of purity and perfection. Lotus flowers grow out of mud but seem untouched by the grime—a symbol used to describe the birth of Buddha, born into the world but not dragged down by it. The lotus also symbolizes summer and fruitfulness.

Mint: Having mint in your garden or in your house attracts money and prosperity *Qi.*

Oleander: A poisonous plant, in China oleander roots are used for medicinal purposes. The oleander is a symbol of beauty and gracefulness.

Onion: The onion is native to southwest Asia. It is used in many parts of the world to guard against evil, presumably due to its very strong smell.

Orchid: Many varieties of orchid are indigenous to China where the blossoms are highly prized. Orchids are symbols of refined beauty, fertility and success.

Peony: A very popular flower in China, the peony is the symbol of spring and feminine beauty. A tree full of flowers is a symbol of good fortune; if the flowers turn an unpleasant color it is a sign trouble is on the way.

Rice: Rice, of course, has become a food staple in China. For this reason the lore of rice is rich and detailed. Sheaves of rice thrown on the roof would protect a house from danger, a jar of rice by the door protects the house from poverty and rice is thrown at weddings to bring wealth to the couple.

Rose: As this flower has thorns, roses should not be planted too close to a garden path, walkway or the entrance to a home.

The thorns will grab at the people who dwell there, creating disharmony in the family. But planted in the garden roses attract love while protecting your heart. Just as a person can't handle a rose roughly for fear of being pierced by the thorns nor can they be careless with the delicate flower of your heart.

Rosemary: Rosemary will improve your memory. Having rosemary in your garden will help you sleep, and give you peaceful, happy dreams.

Sage: Sage is important as a cleansing herb. Many cultures around the world burn sage leaves to cleanse the *Qi* within the home (see section on Clearing, pp. 133). Sage is said to extend life and protect from the evil eye. However, it is also said to be bad luck for you yourself to plant sage in your own garden—find someone else to plant it for you.

Thyme: A wonderfully fragrant herb, it is said that having thyme planted in the garden brings courage. It is also believed to bring a deep, peaceful sleep, without nightmares.

Trees

Trees add beauty and balance wherever they grow and are very important in Feng Shui. They gather *Qi* and create oxygen for us to breath. The history and lore of trees in Chinese culture is as vast as it is in Western cultures and mythology. In ancient times, people both in China and in the West worshipped trees and the spirits that resided in them. Trees were sacred and it was forbidden to cut down certain types of trees that grew in special places. It was believed that certain trees make an area sacred. Today there is a need to protect and cherish trees—our very lives depend on it.

Each variety of tree has its own lore and meaning; it would be impractical to try to cover all of the varieties here. I do, however, want to provide a bit of information about some of the trees that have special meaning to us and special meaning in Feng Shui.

Deciduous trees represent growth and life *Qi*. Having trees in your yard brings *Qi* for personal growth, career expansion, wealth building as well as the potential for health and personal well–being. Even though deciduous trees are bare in winter, they are still alive. So, having these trees in your yard is considered a blessing to the area from the Feng Shui perspective; they gather much–needed *Qi*.

Fruit or nut bearing trees are symbols of abundance since they are producing the gift of food. They bring good luck for career and financial prospects. Whether you gather the fruit of the tree or not, the tree itself is gathering good *Qi* for your home and family.

Evergreen trees are symbols of perseverance and steadfastness. They attract a *Qi* of balance and stability. Evergreen trees stay green through the long, cold winters symbolizing prosperity even in lean times.

Here is specific information about various kinds of trees you might have in your yard:

Apple: Apple trees are not native to China but when they arrived on the scene they became very special to the Chinese people. In Chinese the word for *apple* and the word for *peace* are similar, so having an apple tree in your yard is like inviting peace into your home.

Apricot: Unlike the apple tree, apricots are native to China. The stone or seed of the fruit is said to resemble the eye of a Chinese beauty. The tree adds the *Qi* of abundance as well as beauty to your residence. If there is an apricot tree in front of the house, legend says that you will have beautiful children.

Beech: This tree is not native to China but, according to European lore, it is the guardian of books and wisdom.

Birch: Another tree of mostly European origin, it is said that if you hang red ribbons from the tree, it will protect the house from storms.

Cherry: The fruit of this tree, like that of the apricot, is compared to a woman's beauty. This tree brings the energy of beauty, abundance and joy.

Chestnut: A very large tree that attracts an abundance of *Qi*. Since it is also a nut–bearing tree, it signals fertility and wealth for all who live near its branches.

Elm: Elm is another very large tree that attracts lots of positive *Qi*. In addition, this tree helps the inhabitants of the house by forewarning of disaster. Should it lose its leaves before fall (or earlier than others of its kind in the neighborhood), trouble is on its way.

Eucalyptus: Native to Australia, this is regarded as a healing tree. The Qi attracted by this tree will help support the health of all household members, as well as enhance their overall sense of well–being.

Holly: Found in western Asia and many other parts of the world, holly's nickname is "the warrior tree." The tree is said to guard a house from lightning, poison and evil spirits.

Hawthorn: A native of northern Africa, this tree may also be called the "thorn tree." Despite that, it is said to bring fertility to where it is planted.

Hazel: A special tree found in the United States, the hazel tree was believed to help one see one's way into the future, assisting people to both anticipate opportunity and avoid disaster.

Magnolia: Magnolia is called the "flower that welcomes spring." It brings joy and happiness when planted near a home.

Mulberry: Highly prized in China, the mulberry tree produces edible fruit and also leaves that provide a tasty dinner for silkworms. This tree confers blessings of comfort on the family and helps people find work they love. Mulberry trees are sometimes grown near bamboo, a traditional pair symbolizing honor to one's parents, mother is represented by mulberry; father, bamboo.

Oak: Oak trees are important symbols in China and other parts of the world. Silkworms like the oak leaves as much as mulberry leaves, but the silk produced from the oak is brown, not white. This tree represents masculine (Yang) strength and manhood. Having an oak tree in your garden attracts good and powerful men and gives women as sense of personal power.

Orange: Orange trees are prized both for the food they produce and for medicinal purposes. Since ancient times, the Chinese believed that the orange tree brought good fortune, happiness and prosperity.

Palm: Palm trees are a symbol of happy retirement.

Peach: Said to have originated in China, there is much lore about the peach. In stories dating back 3,000 years, it is identified as a symbol of immortality, it's associated with gods happily feasting on peaches and beautiful maidens turning into peaches. To add prosperity, good *Qi* and energy for a long life, plant a peach tree in your yard.

Pear: Pear trees are associated with the Duke of Shao who lived around 1050 B.C.E. and was said to be wise, compassionate and fair. From this association, the tree has come to represent wisdom, benevolence and justice.

Persimmon: This tree is considered an emblem of joy.

Pine: Because pine trees are evergreen, they are symbols of longevity and of long–lasting friendships. Pine trees are often found near graves in China—its purpose is to protect the dead from evil spirits. A picture of a stork and a pine branch is a Chinese symbol of longevity.

Plum: The plum is a symbol of winter. It is believed that just gazing on a plum tree will quench one's thirst. Plums represent comfort, abundance and long life.

Poplar: Native to western Asia, the poplar is said to bring money. Some say it offers protection from disease and death to all who live near by.

Pomegranate: One of my personal favorites; I was sorry to leave a lovely young pomegranate tree in my back yard in New Mexico—a gift from special friends. Many stories and traditions surround both the fruit and the tree, both in Western mythology and in Eastern lore. The pomegranate is a symbol of fertility and power, and of opportunities for fame and glory.

Rowan: This tree is known as a symbol of healing and protection. Its branches have been used to dowse for water.

Spruce: This tree belongs to the pine and evergreen family and so therefore is about continued prosperity and success through the long winter months.

Walnut: Walnut is a healing tree. It was said that eating the nuts could cure madness, that wearing the leaves could cure headaches, and receiving a gift of walnuts could make your dreams come true.

Willow: A symbol of spring, the willow is prized for the *Qi* it attracts—humble and gentle. Its presence in the garden is said to expel evil. On the fifth day of the fifth lunar month of the Chinese calendar, willow branches can be hung over the door to protect the house from *sha Qi*. It is considered bad luck to have a willow behind the house because the tree's gentleness might be perceived as frailty, adversely affecting people who live in the house. I rarely advise removing a tree, even if it is in an inconvenient place. Use a small mirror attached to the house to reflect back the energy of the tree. This will allow you to keep your back yard willow with no ill effects on family members.

Yew: The Yew tree is associated with temple lands and church yards. It is said to protect from angry ghosts and that sometimes you can even see "faces" in the peeling trunks. When planted in your yard it is said to protect from evil spirits and mischief makers.

Chapter 12

Moving Cures

Water

Perhaps because water is such an important part of human survival, in many cultures it is associated with money and prosperity. Even our idioms here in the West associate water with money. We want good cash flow, liquid assets rather than frozen, and we place our money in a bank (which is the side of a river). In Feng Shui we also associate water with money. Water symbols can bring or attract wealth Qi.

Consider using pictures of moving water (waterfalls, ocean waves or moving rivers) to decorate and stimulate the flow of money Qi. Avoid pictures of frozen water (ice or snow), or still water (small ponds). Hang these pictures in the kitchen, bathroom, home office, living room or entryway.

Fans

Chinese people have used the fan as a practical device and as a symbol of high rank and goodness (the Chinese word for *fan* sounds like the word for *good*) since ancient times. Fans come in a variety of shapes and sizes, and have varying numbers of ribs. They are often painted with decorative scenes and symbolic pictures. Fans were not only used to cool oneself, but to emphasize verbal communication, send non–verbal messages, and to clarify meaning by using the fan to trace out the characters in the air. The fan was also a special object of Zhong Li Quan, Chief of the Immortals (believed to have lived about 250 B.C.E.). The fan is his emblem—its use was to revive the souls of the dead.

Moving cures help stir up Qi and create more interest, passion and enthusiasm. Fans can be plain or intricately painted but must harmonize with the décor of the house in order to be optimally effective. Hanging fans (i.e., fans hung on a wall) are moving cures even though they usually won't move while mounted to a wall.

Tip: If fans do not enhance your décor, try hanging pictures on the wall in a fan–like pattern. To create this effect most successfully, hang at least five (an odd number looks best) pictures on the wall in an arch like a rainbow. This is an attractive way to display a group of pictures, and they then become a useful moving cure.

The Fish Tank

Fish tanks are a classic Feng Shui cure. I have never seen a Chinese restaurant that did not have a fish tank, a fountain or a picture of moving water. The basic rules for using a fish tank as a Feng Shui cure is that the fish need to be alive and healthy, the tank should have moving water (often created using a pump), it should be kept clean. Goldfish are a very good choice, as gold is the color that represents large sums of money. Goldfish are also hardy and, if well cared for, live a long time. Fish tanks can go in any room except the garage. They also need to be kept away from bright sunlight because it can affect both the fish and the tank.

Be careful when placing your fish tank. Watch for conflicting elements: do not, for instance, place fish tanks near fireplaces, wood–burning stoves or kitchen stoves. Water conflicts with fire (and you don't want the little guys to think they are next on the menu). Try to keep your fish alive. Goldfish are actually pretty hardy and can live up to 25 years. Keep an odd number of fish— odd numbers are Yang numbers and are considered more powerful than Yin (even) numbers.

A fish tank should not be in the line of sight of one who is working. It may be very relaxing to sit and watch the fish swim to and fro, but it can be very distracting while trying to work. When placing a fish tank in the home office, the tank should be situated behind the desk. Fish tanks can otherwise be placed in living areas just about anywhere (avoiding the conflicting element factor mentioned above). Fish tanks tend to prosper (and call prosperity *Qi*) if they are kept away from bright light or windows. They also need to be out of the way of traffic areas and play areas.

Beta, or Japanese fighting fish, are small, brightly colored, air–breathing fish you can pick up at the pet store for very little money. A pump is not required with their tanks because they are air breathers. While this type of tank is not as effective at bringing in money *Qi*, it is better than not having a fish tank at all. Since the beta are fighting fish and very territorial, place them in areas where you need to be a bit more aggressive—such as your home office or exercise room. Beta are also good for children who need lots of energy for academics or sports.

Fish tanks are a combination of living moving cures, so they bring growth *Qi* as well as health *Qi*. If you are not up for all of the work involved with the care of the fish and the maintenance of the tank, try a fountain. While not a living cure, a fountain does represent moving water, which attracts good cash flow and wealth.

Fountains

Fountains are even more versatile than fish tanks and require a lot less maintenance. Small, inexpensive fountains can be found everywhere these days. Make sure the one you choose has a pleasant sound (the sound should not send you running to the bathroom). Be careful of fountains that splash; while they are damaging your furniture they are also letting your money *Qi* escape. Fountains should run a few hours each day to effectively attract good money *Qi*. Take care to keep your fountain in good working order, should it stop working, remove it immediately—never allow a non-working fountain to negatively affect your *Qi*.

Flags

Flags, mobiles and kites are moving cures. They help circulate and speed up *Qi*. When people living in the house experience excessive tiredness, laziness or apathy, moving *Qi* is extremely helpful. Moving cures are also good for quiet children, ones who seem shy or frightened of what is going on around them. Use moving cures when you want to change jobs, residences or relationships. Moving cures help get things "unstuck" so you can move forward towards your goals.

Outdoor Flags are very popular right now. Colorful flags can be seen flying in neighborhoods all over the country. These attract lots of *Qi* and bring opportunities. Change out your flags regularly, choosing ones that represent things you want to attract into your life. Indoor flags, like pennants, are not as popular as they used to be. However, they are often used to decorate boys' rooms. This is fine as long as the child is not already hyperactive as flags increase energy and activity levels.

Mobiles are sculptures that move and are usually hung from the ceiling, set on a tabletop or set on the floor. There are a wide variety of fun and attractive perpetual motion sculptures available in many price levels. These sculptures represent the idea of perpetual motion, continuous movement at a steady, manageable pace. Excellent results can be achieved when they are placed in offices and study areas. Mobiles are often hung over cribs to stimulate babies' minds and reflexes. This is fine as long as the mobile is made of a light material—remember not to hang anything heavy over a child's head.

Kites, used by the Chinese for centuries, make interesting wall art. They also represent moving energy, that feeling of reaching for the stars while having fun. These are great cures to hang in family rooms, sunrooms and playrooms.

Chapter 13

Heavy Cures

Crystals

Crystals have several specific uses in Feng Shui and different types of crystals are used for different things. First, allow me to define the two basic types of crystals. The first is a natural crystal, also called a gemstone, that can be in a rough, mineral–grade form, or can be polished, cut or carved. There are a wide variety of crystals in this category and they are used to attract Qi, to ground Qi and to direct Qi. The second type is the prismatic crystal. This is often a piece of leaded glass, usually multi–faceted. When light hits the crystal, the glass acts like a prism breaking the light into a rainbow of colors. These crystals come in many shapes and several colors— each having a specific use and preferred placement. The crystals in this category are usually used to focus or move Qi (see prismatic crystals, pp. 141).

Over thousands of years, the lore of natural crystals and their various properties has been handed down; you will find many books on this subject. The lore is sometimes based on the shape in which the crystal has grown, the color and quality of the crystal or where it was found, but often it consists simply of stories that have been passed down from ancient times.

Diamonds, stones reputed to make one wealthy, are as popular in the United States as anywhere in the world. Today we wear diamonds to signify wealth and status. The actual value of each stone is based on cut, clarity, carat, and color, and these factors determine price. However, inexpensive or even mineral–quality diamonds can be had at good prices. A diamond makes an excellent crystal cure and is your best choice for attracting money. Collecting, wearing or displaying a small diamond or two will help bring money Qi. If that is not feasible, consider purchasing some inexpensive diamond dust or chips and displaying them in a bowl.

Cinnabar is a purple–red to brown–red derivative of mercury. In the fourteenth century alchemists believed they could miraculously transform ordinary metals into silver and gold with the help of this beautiful mineral. In Feng Shui this stone is used to attract wealth and good luck. The red resin statues of Buddha and the dragons that are so popular are colored red to simulate cinnabar. Though cinnabar itself should be placed in the home office, statues made to look like they are cinnabar should be placed according to what they depict, e.g., Quan Yin in the bedroom, dragons protecting the door, etc.

Jade is associated with long life and good health. The English name originates from the Spanish, *piedra de ijada,* literally translated, "stone of the side"—jade was believed to cure kidney ailments if applied to the side of the body. Jade actually refers to two distinct types of stone, both of which closely resemble one another—the more common nephrite and the more expensive jadeite. Jade is harder than granite and more difficult to carve than stolid steel.

When diamonds were first introduced to China sometime between 1000 and 200 B.C.E., they were originally more highly valued as jade–carving tools than as gems. Jade, the "stone of heaven," became so desirable to the Chinese emperors that Confucius even wrote that men should aspire to its qualities of benevolence, intelligence, righteousness, humility, resonance, loyalty, faith, virtue and truth. Today we use jade in the kitchen, the bathroom and the bedroom. If jade is carved into a form, the form dictates placement.

Quartz is another useful stone in Feng Shui. As we know from scientific studies, quartz accumulates energy; it has been used in our watches, clocks and radios for years. Quartz comes in many colors, but the most useful is the clear or white quartz. Quartz comes in several forms, the most useful in Feng Shui being the single terminated, double terminated and tumbled forms. Single–terminated quartz means that one end of the crystal comes to a point while the other end is rough. Double–terminated quartz has a point at both ends. Tumbled quartz is round and smooth like a little, tiny egg. The single–terminated quartz is primarily used as if it were a laser pointer, directing *Qi* where you want it to go.

Double–terminated crystals funnel, accelerate and direct *Qi*. These crystals are best used in long hallways, to move *Qi* up stairways, or to direct *Qi* along an extended road. Tumbled crystals function more like a light bulb than a laser beam. They light up an area the way a "For Sale" sign makes a house more noticeable from the street or the way a sign designates a specific business. Tumbled crystals can be set in the ground with the tops showing near a sign or in a location to attract energy.

Quartz crystals come in many colors. Rose quartz has a pink hue and I have often seen it used for attracting love however it is better for attracting sleep and relaxation. Using it for a relationship cure can attract a lover who is slow, passive and even disinterested. It can be successfully used in a bedroom and it also works well in the family room where family members want to gather peacefully.

The powerful smoky quartz is gray/brown in color. It attracts strong Qi that can help you become an expert, a respected figure in your field. It can bring honor to your career and great status.

Rutilated quartz is a clear quartz with gold or silver "threads" running through it. This is a lucky stone because of the gold or silver threads; it can attract money Qi. Place this stone in your home office or near your front entrance for best results.

Amethyst, purple in color, is a popular and familiar form of quartz. It takes its name from a maiden in Greek mythology who was turned to stone by the god Dionysus. The myth is that Dionysus, in a fit of drunken despair, spilt wine on the maiden–stone, turning it a rich purple. Despite such an unsavory beginning, amethyst is a beautiful stone and can be placed in study areas, meditation areas or near home altars.

There are too many stones to cover them all here but here are a few more that are specifically useful for certain areas of the home.

Petrified Wood is a form of chalcedony that has survived the petrifaction process. During petrifaction, the "wood" is replaced by chalcedony—also known as agate or onyx, depending on the type of banding in the stone. Petrified wood is also an excellent cure around family photos. It brings stability and respect to family relationships so it is best placed in the family room.

Garnet: The name *garnet* comes from the word "grantum" (a type of pomegranate) because of the color resemblance to the seeds of this fruit. Garnets attract a love worth having, keeping, or it can strengthen an existing relationship. Garnet can also protect the heart, making it easier to get into and stay in a relationship.

Amber is not really a gemstone, it is a fossilized resin. Known to mineralogists as succinite, it has a warm, golden glow and is much lighter (by weight) than a normal gemstone. As sticky resin oozed from ancient pine trees, small insects, plant material, feathers and other tiny objects were entrapped in the path of the flow. Over time the resin was encased in dirt and debris and through a process of heat and pressure it fossilized, becoming amber. (The incense copal is un–fossilized amber.)

In China it is believed that when a tiger dies its soul resides in amber until a new tiger is born. Amber is worn as a protective stone. Place amber in the kitchen, bathroom and bedroom to bring longevity, courage and strength.

Moonstone was very popular among the Romans who thought it to be actual beams of moonlight captured within a gem. In India it was and still is considered a sacred gemstone. Moonstones come in a variety of colors and hues, some range from colorless to silver, others are yellow, green, pink or blue. Moonstone is a wonderful Feng Shui cure for enhancing intuition and encouraging people to communicate their feelings with one another. It is best placed in the living room, kitchen or bedroom.

Bloodstone is a dark green/greenish–blue chalcedony with small red, blood–like flecks. Its history can be traced back more than 3,000 years to Egypt and Babylon. It was carried by people who wished to overcome their enemies, open locks and even break prison bonds. However, it is most famous for its reputed ability to stop bleeding. The stone would be placed on a wound, pressure was applied and the bleeding would indeed stop. Bloodstone cures belong in the home office and living room.

Enhydro Crystals contain fluid—most often water—that has remained unchanged and pure for eons. Because of the water contained within the crystal, this specimen stimulates wealth *Qi* and can be placed in the home office or in the kitchen to attract money.

Lapis Lazuli with its deep blue color and flecks of gold, is a mixture of calcite, lazurite and pyrite. Ever since the pharaohs of Egypt, this stone has been associated with royalty. Easily found in jewelry or mineral specimens, it should be placed in areas of the home where you want personal power, near the home computer, in study areas or in the kitchen.

Ruby is a red, gem variety of corundum. The word for ruby derives from the Latin term *rubeus,* meaning red. So enchanted were the ancient Hindus by rubies, they considered them to be *ratnaraj,* the "king of precious stones." In ancient lore the ruby could protect you from enemies: it would grow dark when treachery was near. The ruby should be placed in the south part of the house to protect the family's reputation and standing in the community. Rubies are expensive, however, inexpensive mineral specimens work just as effectively as the pricey cut and polished stones. They should be placed in the living room, family room or home office.

Other Materials

Carved Bone can be used in limited quantities in the home as a cure. We commonly find carved bone in the form of statues or jewelry, the shape dictates placement. A bone statue of Quan Yin, for example, would go in the bedroom. Though the bone itself—a symbol of endings—would not cause a relationship to break up, the combination of bone and Quan Yin's *Qi* would cause it to change. With this in mind, use caution when placing objects made of bone.

Natural bone, especially an animal skull, is generally not good Feng Shui. However, if you are drawn to this type of décor, they can have their place. Bones of dead animals remind us that life is transitory. Placing bones as décor will bring this understanding to you. In other words, you will be provided with opportunities to learn about letting go. Animals bones should only temporarily be placed in an area to bring change to your life. This is a radical step, use it only if you really want something to end! Place bones in your bedroom if you want your current relationship to pass out of your life. Place them in the home office if you really want to let go of your job. The only area where you can safely place bones for long periods is in the spiritual or meditation areas of the house. There the bones will attract ancient wisdom from masters who have long ago passed into the pages of history.

Sea Shells: Interest in sea shell collecting is gaining popularity. There are so many beautiful shapes, colors and kinds of shells. These reminders of the sea help us stimulate *Qi* that brings greater stability to our careers, and protects the wealth of the family. The particular type of shell is not as important as the condition; use only whole shells, not pieces. The more spiky and pointy the shell is, the more aggressive the financial protection. If you wish to change careers choose smooth shells, like *cowrie,* to make the transition uneventful. If you need to protect your current position or job, choose a spiky shell, such as a *murex.*

Gold and Silver: Metals like gold and silver stimulate wealth *Qi,* even when used in very small quantities. Gold attracts larger sums of money and is a good cure to have in the home office, near the front door and in the living room. If you cannot afford a gold coin or piece of jewelry, consider gold leaf as a possibility. Gold leaf kits are available at craft stores and you could apply the leaf to a bowl, vase or even a piece of furniture.

Silver attracts money in smaller amounts, and will encourage people to spend money on you. Since silver is nearly white in color, it can be placed in children's rooms to help your children prosper in all that they do. Besides selecting objects plated in silver as decorative touches, consider acquiring some silver coins (these can be very affordable). Place silver coins on the window sill in the home office or near the front door to attract financial and monetary opportunities.

Clearing Crystals

When we use crystals to move *Qi,* we want that crystal to be clear of any *sha Qi* and anyone else's personal energy. If you have ever held a crystal in your hand and felt a tingling or vibrating sensation in your palm, you are feeling the energy of that crystal. When you touch a crystal and feel as though you don't want to put it down, rather you want to hold it and explore it with your fingers, you are feeling the energy of that particular crystal. When you buy a crystal from your local merchant, the crystal will have stored some of the *Qi* of the store where you bought it, of the people who harvested it, shipped it or handled it before you touched it. Likewise if you receive a crystal as a gift from a friend, it will carry some of their energy. When you are not sure about the energy your crystal carries, it is best to cleanse it before placing it as a cure.

You can choose one of five methods—based on the five Chinese elements—to cleanse your crystal. You can cleanse using water, fire, earth, metal or wood. To cleanse by water, simply wash your crystal in good, pure water and dry thoroughly. To cleanse by fire, smudge the crystal with burning sage. (Smudging is a Native American method of clearing an object or a space. See *"Sage & Smudge: Secrets to Clearing Your Personal Space"* in the bibliography.) To cleanse the crystal by earth, bury the crystal in good soil for twenty–four hours. You may choose to do this in a pot or in your yard, just don't forget where you put it. To cleanse by metal, take a brass bell or set of bells and ring them loudly around the crystal. Sound clears *Qi* very effectively. And finally, a clearing by wood involves placing the crystal in some lavender— either growing or cut—for twenty–four hours. Lavender is a cleansing herb, in fact the name itself means, "to wash."

Once the crystal is cleansed, consecrate it. *Consecration* is a fancy word for assigning a purpose to something, it's like giving the crystal a job to do. When something has been consecrated, it cannot be used for any other purpose; when it has a job, it is more effective because it devotes all its energy to that purpose. (Should you ever want to use the crystal for another purpose, then cleanse it and re–consecrate it.)

For example, to consecrate a crystal to stimulate career *Qi* to bring you a new opportunity with another company, take the cleansed crystal in your hand and say aloud, in a firm voice, "the purpose of this crystal is to help me locate a better job—one that brings me more money, greater job satisfaction and potential for future promotion." Then place the crystal in the spot designated by the rules of Feng Shui.

After placing the crystals you may soon notice remarkable changes in your life. But then after a month or so it may seem that things slow down again. Like a battery, your crystals need an occasional recharge. Simply cleanse and re–consecrate the crystal then return it to its place. Sometimes it may be necessary to actually replace a crystal with a new one, but usually a crystal will recharge many times before this is necessary.

Chapter 14

Scent Cures

Oils and Incense

Scent—oils, incense and candles—changes the *Qi* by changing the scent of a room. Smell is one of our most intense senses; a specific scent can invoke memory and has the power to change our mood. Scent attracts and brings new *Qi* into any environment. We can use scented candles, burning them to disburse fragrance in the room. We can light incense, using it solely to infuse the air with its aroma. What we need to remember is that any scent we choose will activate *Qi*, so it is important to choose one that will be in harmony with the type of energy you want to attract. A variety of books are available on the subject of scent that explore the meaning and lore behind each. Here are some tips to get you started:

Cedar: Cedar is a very woodsy, almost spicy scent and helps you ground yourself and connect to the earth in a spiritual sense.

Chamomile: This herb offers a full–bodied scent, almost fruity in essence. It brings peace and is known to support a meditative frame of mind and encourage slumber.

Cinnamon: Many of us recognize the scent of cinnamon from the baking and holiday celebrations of our childhood and youth. It is a warm, spicy scent that could trigger a desire for holiday fare. Traditionally this fragrance was used to attract money and wealth. (Caution: Cinnamon oil can burn the skin, so use sparingly in this form.)

Clove: Clove is another of our holiday favorites that we can now enjoy any time of year. In olden days, men wore this scent to give themselves courage and strength. (Caution: Clove oil can burn the skin, so use sparingly in this form.)

Frankincense: Used for centuries, and said to be one of the gifts brought to the Christ child by the Three Magi, frankincense has served in many rituals of a variety of world religions. It is believed to promote spirituality and meditation.

Ginger: Ginger has a very spicy aroma and is said to have aphrodisiac qualities.

Jasmine: A lightly sweet, flower fragrance that attracts a peaceful, precious love into your life.

Lavender: Found in gardens around the world, lavender has a clean, refreshing scent. This fragrance is used to cleanse any area of negativity.

Lemon: A citrus and sharp scent often used for cleansing and purifying.

Myrrh: Offers a scent as sweet and thick as good syrup, myrrh can be used for healing. A combination of myrrh and frankincense attracts wealth.

Orange: A citrus and sweet aroma that balances *Qi*, especially relationship *Qi*.

Patchouli: A woodsy, almost medicinal scent which has traditionally been used to attract love, money and anything else your heart may desire.

Pine: A woodsy, resinous aroma that reminds us of the forests and of winter, commonly used for cleansing and purifying.

Rose: Around the world this scent is considered to be the perfect floral—not too sweet, not too heavy. It is the classic scent for attracting love.

Sandalwood: The scent of far–away places and mysterious pathways, sandalwood has been used since ancient times to promote creativity and invite peace.

Vanilla: The sweet, delicious fragrance of the vanilla bean can bring back memories of happy times. It is used to quickly attract love and good fortune.

Diffusing Oils

There are two basic types of oils. "Essential oil" refers to the essence of the plant itself. Usually extremely expensive, one only needs a tiny amount of an essential oil to scent a room. "Perfume oils" are synthetic or a blend of both essential and synthetic oils. These are usually less expensive but more is needed to achieve the same level of scent.

In times past essential oils were preferred because they are derived from the actual plant itself. However, over time some plants have become scarce and synthetic oils have been created that smell so authentic that it is hard to differentiate them from their essential oil counterparts. Synthetic musk oil is always preferable to the real thing because essential musk oil is derived from the sweat glands of the male musk deer, many are killed each year for this purpose.

A diffuser is usually in the form of a candleholder with a bowl on top. You can add a drop or two of the chosen oil to the bowl, and light a tea candle (a small candle in a metal holder) underneath. The candle warms the oil, diffusing the scent into the room. However, you can also diffuse oils in boiling water. Bring some water to the boil and simply add a few drops of the preferred scented oil. Allow the water and oil to boil a few moments, then remove from the heat. An old realtor's trick is to diffuse a bit of vanilla in boiling water before showing a house in order to attract a buyer.

You can also diffuse oils simply by pouring a drop or two on a cotton ball and leaving it in the room. If you are using this method, place the cotton ball on a plate or in a small bowl as some oils can stain furniture.

Stick incense is a combustible incense. The incense is adhered to a wooden skewer and diffuses as the wood in the stick burns. Often these incenses are oil–based but it is possible to find pure resin incense in stick form (you can tell it's pure because the price is considerably higher). A very small amount of potassium nitrate has been added to the incense as a combustion agent, this allows the incense to burn.

To burn stick incense, light the tip and watch it flame briefly. When the tip glows, gently blow out the flame and place the stick in an incense holder. To extinguish the stick, grind out the tip in a fireproof container. Burning time varies from a few minutes to an hour and a half, depending on the type of stick you have chosen to burn.

Cone incense, also combustible, is formed into the shape of a cone. The only difference between stick incense and cone is there is no wooden skewer. Most cone incense is oil based. To use cone incense, light the top of the cone and place it on a fireproof plate.

When the tip glows, blow out the flame. (Blow very gently or you may send the flaming cone flying.) Cones burn anywhere from a few minutes to an hour.

In its most natural state, incense is non–combustible. It must be provided with a heat source—like charcoal—in order to burn. Resin incenses are the best example of a natural incense. You can also use the spices in your cupboard as incense—they can be burned or smoldered.

Resin incense: Most stores that sell resin incense will also sell charcoal which is necessary for diffusing the scent. This charcoal comes in small discs, often treated so they will light quickly. Hold the charcoal disc carefully with tongs and light with a match or lighter. Place the charcoal disc in a fireproof container or in a bowl filled with sand. The disc will sparkle and smoke slightly as it is lit. Place one–half teaspoon of incense on the lit charcoal disc. Non–combustible incenses have a very strong scent and there may be a lot of smoke, so use this type of incense sparingly.

Other Incense: Incense comes in several more shapes and sizes. Rope incenses, coils and incense pressed into shapes are all available. These are combustible incenses. Some incenses are specially blended for a specific purpose, others are single scents as described above. Try some to discover your own preference. For the beginner, let me recommend Nag Champa, a floral scent that is probably the most popular and best–selling in the world. It is said to bring joy.

Chapter 15

Color Cures

Using color is probably the quickest and most effective way to change the Qi in a room. Each color has its own wavelength and scientific studies show that color impacts our physiology. Psychologists tell us that each color evokes a singular emotion and that the colors themselves represent universal feelings. The right choice of color can either energize us or cause us to relax, it can strengthen us or make us tired, it can elevate our mood or literally sedate us. It has even been suggested that "color–blind" people are affected by color.

Color evokes feeling. The feeling may not be easy to articulate but the emotion is there. Some people are highly sensitive and react to slight changes in color while others respond only to strong shifts in color. Different cultures associate colors with different things but the effect of the color is the same. We, in the United States, associate the color red with fire engines, stop signs and other attention–getting symbols. In other cultures red still attracts attention but represents different things. Red gives us the impression of energy, movement and excitement.

Red is a favorite color for the Chinese, especially a bright, clear red. This color is considered lucky, happy, and it serves to attract good fortune. The color red is used for all festive occasions. Chinese characters are inscribed on red streamers and hung outside homes at New Year to welcome fortune.

Red is the color associated with the direction south; from a Feng Shui perspective, if you have a south–facing door, it is a good idea to paint it red. South walls in the house can also be red. The color red is associated with the fire element and can therefore be used when you need to encourage enthusiasm.

Use red to either attract Qi into a room or to focus people's attention on some point or area in the room. It can also be used to draw people's attention away from some other aspect of the décor or architecture you don't want them to notice. Red can be used in any room of the house but it is a particularly excellent choice in the bedroom as it enhances and stimulates relationship Qi. Use red near the front door to invite luck into your life and use it in the kitchen—the power center of the house—to focus more energy towards cooking and nurturing you and your family.

Color should always be used in a balanced manner. If there is too much of one color in a space, negative aspects of the emotions and feelings represented by that color can surface. How much is too much? Well, it's hard to say. The amount varies with the size of the room and the use of the space. A bedroom with red walls and a red bedspread, for instance, may promote passion in your relationship, but it is not very conducive to sound sleep habits. Too much red and the people who live in the space may become short–tempered or aggressive with one another. Red can stimulate anger. The Chinese say that a red sky symbolizes warfare, and even here in the West we have an old saying, "red sky in morning, sailors take warning," meaning, a red sky is a sign that a storm is brewing.

Blue is the color of heaven according to Chinese tradition. It is the color of the sky, of the ocean, of rivers and lakes. Blue is associated with expansiveness, lofty thinking, the future we hope to create and an awareness of the impact individual choices and decisions have on the world. We can add blue when we wish to symbolize wisdom or the power of the mind, when we wish to travel or feel free of our earthly limitations. We can also use the color blue to enhance feelings of confidence or the conviction of our beliefs.

In China, the color blue is considered a very respectable color, often worn as a symbol of an educated person. Blue is associated with the water element in Feng Shui (as is black, which we will discuss in more detail). The color blue enhances communication and good social contacts. It encourages people to have mutual respect for one another. Choose this color in bedrooms, kitchens and living areas. It can be used on walls or to highlight specific areas of a room. It is the ideal color to use in areas where you want to study and remember what you have learned.

Too much blue will attract some of the negative associations we have with this color. When people are "blue," they are sad and melancholy; they may feel tired or depressed. Too much blue can make a room or a space feel cool, even cold—not welcoming and homey.

Yellow is the national color of China (bet you thought red was). Yellow was the color of the emperor's robes and is still associated with high rank and power. Palace roofs are often yellow. Charms to ward off evil spirits are printed on yellow paper and hung from trees and porch posts. And the Chinese say that when you see a yellow sky, prosperity is on its way.

Yellow is a color that helps us remember the past. Think of all of the things we Westerners associate with the color yellow: our phone book's yellow pages, the yellow school bus, and yellow legal pads. Yellow is the color of history, memory and learning. It represents friendship and mutual respect. Sunny yellow comes in a multitude of shades, ones we can use to bring light into our lives. This spectrum includes yellow mixed with brown to give us more of a dark, mustard yellow, or yellow mixed with green to bring us bright, springtime chartreuse.

In the Chinese system of elements, yellow is associated with earth and represents stability and balance. Having this color in your environment helps you to feel grounded. Decorate with yellow when you want to enhance your practical abilities and your common sense. Use shades of yellow in your study, in the den, in living spaces and in bathrooms. Some say the color yellow can stimulate hunger, so they avoid using it in the kitchen. If you are wanting to diet, stay out of a yellow kitchen. However, to increase your energy and industry in the kitchen (and to help you make wonderfully delicious and healthy meals) consider at least some yellow accents in that room.

What negative energy could possibly be associated with the color yellow, you ask? Negative feelings such as fear, nervousness, apprehension and guilt are most commonly associated with the color. Yellow doesn't create them, but it can bring existing feelings to the surface.

These are the three primary colors. They blend to make the secondary colors: green, orange and purple.

Green is a blend of blue and yellow. Green is associated with growth, prosperity and wellness. Picture a deep green valley with rolling hills of green grass and leaf–filled trees; this is the feeling of health. Even if this is not your ideal picture, the image conjures up feelings of wellness and prosperity. In the United States our money is green—so, as a nation, we further associate green with wealth.

In other countries where multi–colored money is exchanged, different emotions and feelings are associated with currency. Here in the United States, however, we have one wish for our money: that it grow and be as abundant as the leaves on a tree.

In China green is worn by officials of lower rank. Green is associated with east, the direction of the sacred dragon. In Feng Shui, green is associated with the wood element. This element represents growth and family, maintaining good health and having a lifestyle that promotes well–being. The Chinese look to the wood element to support healthy relationships with family members— however close or distant they may be. As a color choice, green works in most rooms of the house. But, it is particularly beneficial in the bedroom, the room where we rest, recuperate and heal from the challenges of our day. Green in the family room helps promote harmonious communication between the members of the family. And any shade of green is positive in a home office because it can stimulate productivity and cash flow *Qi*.

The negative expression of green is an interesting one. In China, green is the color of the painted sign that criminals carry on their way to meet the executioner. It is said that seeing a green sky means that a plague of insects is coming. Too much green in the décor can bring up issues of envy; this can lead to an overall dissatisfaction with life. It can cause unfavorable comparisons between you and your perception of how the rest of the world sees you. When you use green in your décor, try to balance it with several colors in order to achieve a harmonious ambiance.

White is the color created when all colors of the spectrum are combined, it represents a blend of any and all feelings and emotions. Clarity is also represented by the color white. For a moment, think how obvious a blemish on a white wall can be—this is the type of clarity white brings to a situation. White also represents holding on, retaining something until you have decided whether you want to keep it or not. White is the basic and most popular color we use to decorate our homes here in the West. No surprise, we tend to hold very tightly onto our things. If you have a clutter problem, you will find that it is easier to let go if you are not surrounded by white walls.

The metal element in the Chinese system is the one associated with the color white, as is the direction west. In Feng Shui, this element governs children, creativity and our own child–like qualities. The color white can help stimulate creativity—anything from music and art to crafts to basic home improvement. White provides a blank canvas for the expression of creative ideas. The metal element also pulls the kind of *Qi* we need to take care of our possessions, the material aspects of life; it helps us to stay safe in our environment and achieve a balance between work and play.

In China white is the color worn to funerals. The color allows the Chinese to hold memories of those who have passed on and to keep them in their lives. Actors on a Chinese stage will paint their faces white to denote a character who is dignified on the outside but treacherous on the inside—white hides the character's sinful nature.

When we are surrounded by too much white, we can feel the need to be perfectionists or to cover our own flaws with a wall of white, living a life hidden behind a social mask. You may even become afraid to show your true nature out of fear that others will reject you when a blemish is found. This leads to feelings of isolation and a contracting of the social circle.

Black is the color of power and protection; it is both loved and feared in the same way that we love the blanket of night, yet fear the dark. In many cultures black has symbolized evil, darkness and secrecy, but it is also our fashion friend, the slimming classic that is never the wrong color. Black allows us a little breathing room, creating a boundary between us and the rest of the world. With all of the protection offered by black, it is no wonder this color is a fashion choice for teenagers and young people in our modern, scary world. After all, the young can fear everything from relationships to what the future holds for them—and they want as much distance as possible from everything and everyone. Black is also the color of power. This concept is so deeply ingrained in our psyche that when we see a person dressed in a black suit, we immediately assume they are in charge.

In Feng Shui black is associated with the water element. The darkness signifies the mysteries of the ocean depths. Black, with blue, is also associated with the north, the darkest of directions. Black can be used sparingly in décor. Black accents call power *Qi* and are especially beneficial in business and home office areas. Black provides a protective barrier and can be used near the front door if you feel unsafe for any reason in your home. It is also considered an acceptable color to paint the walls of a media or entertainment room as it enhances the viewing enjoyment when people watch movies or other on–screen entertainment. Otherwise, unless one is decorating a trendy retail store, painting rooms black is considered unlucky.

Black is an unpopular color in China. Its *Qi* is considered to be fierce and warrior–like. There are many sayings both here and in China referring to the color black. For example, "a person with a black heart embraces vice," and black skies bring floods. Too much black and any room becomes a dark cave, uninviting and lonely. Black can isolate us from the rest of the world and negate all of the safety the color otherwise offers. Wear as much black as you like but use the color sparingly in the house.

Purple's positive energy is related to spiritual assistance, understanding and serenity; on the flip side it is associated with physical weakness, being so spiritual that the physical can be ignored. Purple is a wonderful color for attracting spiritual *Qi*, for increasing psychic ability and for attracting the type of people who need your particular expertise. In China purple is worn by the grandsons of ranking officials, denoting that they have some power but they are not in charge. Well–educated people may also wear purple.

Purple can be used to decorate businesses and home offices, especially if the business is owned by service–oriented professionals, such as counselors and doctors, those who assist others with emotional and physical problems. Purple attracts attention and gives the impression of wisdom and other special, intuitive qualities.

If one is surrounded by too much purple, or wears too much purple, awareness of the many aspects of our physical reality are weakened, and we become less grounded (e.g., forgetting to pay bills, neglecting to follow up on opportunities, avoiding exercise and disregarding good eating habits). On the other hand, purple is a good color choice for meditation rooms, craft rooms, and accents in the living room. It is sometimes used in restaurants—but be wary that the food may not feed the body as well as the color feeds the soul.

Violet is a lighter and gentler version of purple. While it has aspects of both red and blue, the *Qi* is muted. It is a superb color to enhance the ability to meditate and can bring peace to a troubled household. It is not considered wise, however, to have a lot of violet or lavender in a room where someone is recovering from an illness. The color does not necessarily enhance physical healing, nor is it strong enough to attract the kind of spiritual help that may be required.

Pink is a very soft version of red and probably most associated with the idea of love or romance. Traditionally this color is used to bring sleep and relaxation. It is a low–energy color and does not encourage action. It can be used to attract a love partner who is pliable and willing to be ruled. (Most people I have met prefer a partner with a bit more energy and confidence so red would be the best color.) Pink is a great color to have around if you are feeling overstressed and have trouble winding down.

Pink is also an effective shield for hiding your power (or desire for power) from others. If you wear pink in the boardroom, you may not be seen as a powerful individual, but you will quietly be able to listen and make plans for the future. If you are going to a meeting where you don't want to appear powerful (this may have some tactical advantages in some situations), try wearing pink. If you are surrounded by too much pink, your potential may be hidden, even from yourself. Avoid pink for a while if you are recovering from an illness, or if you feel low on energy.

Because of the good and more challenging aspects of *Qi* associated with the color pink, consider using it only in the décor in family rooms where it is preferable to keep the peace, or perhaps in the dining room where relaxed harmony may be the goal. Pink bathrooms are fine when the people in the house are healthy, but if people are recovering from illness or have chronic health problems, it is a good idea to re–decorate and have a green bathroom (to promote good health).

Colors like pink are usually preferred in fuchsia tones. These are pinks that have a lot more vibrancy than the traditional pale pinks we are used to here in the West. Pink is still a mixed bag. In English the word *pink* means to cut something with a jagged edge, to stab lightly with a pointed weapon, to have radical, socialist political views. *Pink collar* denoted a job in the secretarial pool, a relatively powerless position. None of these particularly support the Madison Avenue version of the color as one that promotes sweet, romantic love. So, think before you choose pink....

Peach is one of my personal favorite colors. It has all of the relaxing, meditative energy of pink, with a little red/orange energy–kicker to spice up things a little. As a wall or accent color, peach works in most of the rooms of the house—bedrooms in particular—for it will both help you relax to fall asleep and wake up energized. Peach is the perfect color for craft rooms, kitchens and any room where you want to unwind with creative projects.

Orange is another of my favorite colors. It is bright and happy; it brings a sense of adventure and the unexpected to any room. It is the color of enlightenment and assimilation and will help you absorb everything from new knowledge to the vitamins in your food. Orange can be used in a bedroom, kitchen or craft room. It will stimulate all of the positive and uplifting aspects of spending time in that room. Too much orange can become stressful, and bring you more ideas than any one person can possibly complete. If all of the walls in a room are orange, use very strong, contrasting colors for the furnishing and décor. This will add balance to the room.

Burgundy is historically associated with money and power. The color itself is rich and potent, making all who wear it feel strong and more confidently able to connect with opportunities. Add this color to your home office, or to the area around where you work to stimulate the *Qi* to bring profit and benefit. Place a little burgundy near your front door to bring career opportunities.

Brown is a stabilizing color that attracts earthy, grounded and one that is associated with material objects. Most houses have a lot of brown with the hardwood floors, wood furniture, door frames and wooden stairs. All of these add up to an abundance of the color. Here, in the West, we seem to own plenty of material objects, so much so that we most often need to de–clutter rather than attract more.

Too much brown can be so stabilizing that our lives become motionless. For ten years I lived comfortably in the brown landscape of New Mexico, where nearly all of the houses are painted in one of the 28 shades of brown. After a decade of brown on brown, stability had become stagnation and it was hard to move.

Tan and *cream,* antique white and off–white are all a mix of brown and white (sometimes with a hint of yellow). These are the colors of hard work for little reward. A little bit of tan is fine—but room after room of neutral beige walls, brownish rugs, and cream furnishings bring a constant, endless stream of things to do and jobs to finish. Add a little color and create balance in your life.

Gray and *ecru* are power colors, devoid of emotion, they represent pure thought. Think of the color of your computer. It is this color because the company that made it wants you to think that you have the most powerful machine, the one that will solve all of your problems. Gray is good for home offices and areas where you want to feel in charge, to feel powerful.

Taupe is a combination of gray and brown and combines an essence of power with the qualities of industry and thrift. It is an excellent color choice for formal living rooms and home offices.

Dusty Rose is a combination of pink and gray; it calls an energy of softness with logic. This color allows you to process lots of information while concealing your power. It is often seen in corporate offices, both in carpet and upholstered furniture, giving a soft, non–threatening image.

Gold—the metallic variety—is the obvious color of wealth and large sums of money. Add gold to a room by choosing brass objects, metallic paint, gold leaf accents or brass hardware. Of course, real gold works well too, but if you are decorating in real gold, you are already very lucky. Gold can be used in any room of the house, but sparingly in the bedroom unless your goal is to marry for money.

Silver—here again, the metallic variety—is the color of coin representing small sums of money and regular income. Silver can be added to any room using objects made of nickel, steel and, of course, silver. Too much silver in the décor is likely to lead to spending money rather than attracting it. If you find that it is hard to hold onto your cash (or savings) change out some of your silver decorative items for gold–colored ones.

Chapter 16

Symbol Cures

Buddhas and Immortals

Buddhism is a major religion in the world with a message of living in peace and harmony. The little Buddha statues, often recognized as Feng Shui cures, are good luck symbols. People either carry the statues with them or place them in their homes to call *Qi*. However, one does not need to be a Buddhist in order to enjoy the good energy the statues bring. Buddha statues come in many forms. You can choose from the money Buddha, who holds his gold bullion over his head, or the health Buddha wearing his sacred mala necklace or the protection Buddha with his decorative umbrella, each bring their own energy. The following is a list of some of the little Buddha statues, the Immortals (people who gained prominence while alive who were later elevated to the status of immortal) and other important figures and their recommended placement.

Confucius was a sage who lived from 551–479 B.C.E. in China. He was a teacher who believed that people would live better lives if they followed the path of virtue. Confucius' teachings have had an enormous influence on Chinese philosophy, thought and custom. The five virtues he suggested are benevolence, justice, propriety, wisdom and sincerity. If you choose a statue of Confucius, place it on your desk at work to encourage all who enter your space to follow these rules. At home, place it in a teenager's room to encourage diligent studies and respect for the family.

Fuk (Fu) is one of the three immortals (Luk, Fuk and Sau). He is the guardian of wealth. Fuk holds a gold ingot (the *ru–yi*, shaped like a ball on a dish) in his hands and is usually placed between the other two immortals. A good location is in the dining room, though he can also be placed in the living room to bring financial benefit to the family.

Luk (Lu) is the immortal representative of high rank and authority, a protector of children and of the family reputation. Place him near family photographs in the bedroom if you are attempting to become pregnant or in the children's room to protect them. Or, display all three immortals, Luk, Fuk and Sau. (Luk is placed on the left as you face them.)

Sau (Shou) is the third immortal, easily identified by his bald head. He is considered the essence of longevity. Place this cure in the bedroom to bring good luck with health and long life or place the statue in a sickroom to bring healing energy to one who is ill. Or Sau can be displayed with the other two immortals, Luk and Fuk, in the dining room. (Sau should be placed on the right as you face them.)

Gambling Buddha sits with his winning peach, a lucky symbol of abundance, long life and happiness. Carry this one with you if you go gambling; place lottery tickets under this Buddha or put him in the kitchen to bring wealth to the household.

Happiness Buddha is the one we are probably most familiar with; he is shown sitting, displaying his big, round belly and his long ears (a symbol of wisdom). Place the happiness Buddha in the bedroom to help you wake up happy each morning, or place him in the family room to bring joy to the entire family.

Quan Yin (*Guan Yin or Kwan Yin*) is a goddess, said to be the embodiment of loving kindness. She is often depicted pouring a stream of healing waters from a small vase. This statue can be placed near the entrance of a home to bless with spiritual peace all who enter. Quan Yin can be placed in the bedroom to provide *Qi* to draw in a happy, loving relationship.

Quan Yin with her Dragon is a depiction of the goddess of love and mercy with a dragon coiled at her feet. This is a passionate Quan Yin, symbolizing sensuality, strength and vitality. Keep her in the bedroom to enhance your sex life or place her in the living room to attract a new lover.

Money Buddha is the classic, big bellied Buddha, holding a lucky gold ingot over his head. Place him on your desk to attract more money or financial prosperity. Then place any money you receive under this Buddha for twenty–four hours before making your deposit in order to attract even more. Place this Buddha in your living room to attract monetary benefit to the household.

Lord Guan Yu (Guan Gung) was a powerful protector and alchemist—a huge man with a long beard who dedicated his life to his friends. He became a national symbol of loyalty and honor. This statue wards off evil and attracts people who can help you achieve your goals. Carry this representation with you when you need inner strength, or place it near the front door to attract powerful allies.

Protection Buddha sits with his umbrella resting on his shoulder and a cheerful smile on his face. Umbrellas are a symbol of rank and are used to keep evil spirits away from the head/mind. Place this Buddha near the front door to protect the house or place it in the bedroom to protect you while you sleep.

Resting Buddha sits in a contemplative position, holding a fan. Place this Buddha in the family room to help all members of the household relax and maintain clear communications with one another, or keep a statue in the car to help maintain restraint and prevent road rage.

Good Luck Buddha shows the Buddha carrying a sack, reputed to be filled with toys and good things to eat for all the children he meets—much like our western image of Santa Claus. This Buddha also carries a fan, a symbol of art and creativity. Place the good luck Buddha on a map or picture of a desired destination, and you will find a way to get where you want to go; or place him in your car to help you with your travels. Place this Buddha in your craft and hobby area to call *Qi* to support your talents and creative gifts.

All statues of the Buddhas and immortals can also be used on home altars. Buddhas can be anointed with essential oils or perfume oils and placed on the altar when a specific *Qi* is needed and then returned to their regular place as opportunities arrive.

Coins

Chinese coins are unique with their round shape and square hole in the center. They represent both heaven (round) and earth (square). The coins are usually strung together and hung inside or out to protect and bless the house with abundance and wealth. You can use real or replica coins of any type of money all work for the same purpose—to attract riches. Coins can be worn as jewelry to attract money directly into your hands. They are an especially useful cure if you are in business for yourself. Strung together,

Symbol Cures

Fuk, Luk and Sau (from left to right) are the Gods of health, wealth & longevity. In Feng Shui they represent the most important aspects of good fortune.

The Famous Chinese sage, Confucius, was a well-known leader in philosophy and he was also the author of many aphorisms and theories about the law, life, and the government. His symbol promotes virtue and honor.

Quan Yin, the bringer of mercy, is seen as the embodiment of loving kindness. She is sometimes depicted with pearls (of illumination), a vase (of healing water), or a dragon (symbol of transformation and wisdom).

Money Buddha, sometimes called Hotei or the Good Luck Buddha is depicted holding a gold ingot (shaped like a little boat) over his head. It is said that rubbing his belly will bring luck.

coins can be hung in the car to attract prosperity wherever you go. Coins can be placed on a windowsill near the front door to attract good fortune. A silver coin can be placed above the front door, resting on the molding, so the house never lacks for money. Pictures or replicas of money can be used in offices to attract prosperity. Coin cures come in several styles, here are some examples:

Single–coin charms are usually attached to a bell. This charm can be hung anywhere one would hang a wind chime. Hang it outside on the front porch to call money *Qi*, or hang it inside in the place where you either receive money or balance your checkbook to help money accumulate in your accounts.

Three–coin string charms attract people who can assist you financially. Hang three–coin charms near your telephone to make it easy to close business deals or carry this charm with you at business meetings.

Six–coin string charms bring comfort and financial ease. Hang a six–coin charm in the family room so the family can be assured of financial well–being. Or, hang this charm in the kitchen so that money will not be wasted.

Eight–coin string charms are lucky because eight is the Chinese number of happiness. Hang an eight–coin charm and find that all roads lead to money. Hang the charm in the home office for happy career success or hang it by the front door to welcome the monetary opportunities that come knocking.

Eight–coin circle charms represent the ring of happiness. Hang this charm in the space where you pay bills so that the money you pay out always returns with added benefit. What you give out will come back to you, with interest.

Eight–coin jade strings combine the happiness, symbolized by the number eight, with the healing power of jade. This charm is said bring the resources needed when one is ill. Hang this charm on the bedpost or headboard, or hang it in the kitchen to bring healing *Qi* into the house.

Nine–coin strings represent nine of the great emperors of China, who symbolize great glory and wealth. Hang this charm over the front door, or place it with investment materials.

Eighteen–coin strings are called the "never–ending coin strings." They symbolize a never–ending source of income for you and your family. Hang this string charm where you do business or where you do the family finances.

Coin balls consist of many coins tied together with red string to form a ball. This coin ball charm is said to help one finish up business projects and close deals. Hang the charm near your desk or carry it in your car and it will bring business success.

Coin swords are coins tied together to form a sword. This charm protects from poison arrows and the evil intentions of others. Point this sword at the doorway of your home or business for protection.

Other Cures

Gold ingots look like little boats with eggs in them, but this symbol actually represents a Chinese gold bullion. The little boat *(ru–yi)* symbolizes easy sailing—a happy life filled with great abundance. Gold ingot charms can be hung in home offices, in kitchens or in doorways—wherever you hang them, they attract money Qi.

Gourds are a symbol of mystery and magic. They have been used by Chinese pharmacists as their symbol, much in the same way ours use a mortar and pestle. The gourd, which is shaped like a bottle, is often depicted being carried by the benevolent Buddha and is said to be filled with the elixir for eternal youth. It is a symbol for a long and healthy life. Place gourds in the kitchen, bathroom or bedroom.

Lucky Knots symbolize a long life without struggle or setbacks. A series of knots is often translated to mean "an easy ladder to success." Knot charms are hung in study areas, kitchens and work areas. They can also be carried for luck in business.

In conclusion

I am so happy that you have decided to add Feng Shui principles to your life. I have received so many emails, calls and letters from people who have experienced such great results from making even small changes. I encourage you to experiment, and experience the shifts in energy for yourself. And as you create a more healing, balanced environment for you and your family you will be more able to attract the resources you need to have the life you want.

Notes

Notes

Notes

Notes

Bibliography

Anonymous. *Feng Shui: Ancient Secrets for a Lucky Home*. New York: International Rights Ltd., 1996.

Baker, John Milnes, A.I.A. *American House Styles*. New York: W.W. Norton & Company, 1994.

Brown, Simon. *Practical Feng Shui*. London: Wardlock, 1997.

Bruun, Ole. *Fengshui in China*. Honolulu: University of Hawaii Press, 2003.

Carter, Karen Rauch. *Move Your Stuff, Change Your Life*. New York: Fireside, 2000.

Chuen, Master Lam Kam. *Personal Feng Shui Manual*. New York: Henry Holt and Company, 1998.

Craze, Richard with Bill Lee. *Teach Yourself Chinese Astrology*. NTC/ Contemporary Publishing, 1997.

Cunningham, Scott. *Cunningham's Encyclopedia of Magical Herbs*. St Paul, MN: Llewellyn Publications, 1997.

De Mente, Boyé Lafayette. *The Chinese Have a Word for It: Complete Guide to Chinese Thought and Culture*. Lincolnwood, IL: Passport Books, 2000.

Eberhard, Wolfram. *A Dictionary of Chinese Symbols*. London: Routledge, 1986.

Eitel, Ernest. *Feng Shui: The Science of Sacred Landscape in Old China*. Truber & Co, 1873. Reprinted, Tucson, AZ: Synergetic Press, 1984.

Feuchtwang, Stephan. *An Anthropological Analysis of Chinese Geomancy*. Bangkok: White Lotus, 2002.

Groves, Derham. *Feng–Shui and Western Building Ceremonies*. Graham Brash, Singapore and Tynron Press, U.K., 1991.

Hale, Gill. *The Feng Shui Garden*. Pownal, VT: Storey Books, 1998.

——. *The Practical Encyclopedia of Feng Shui*. London: Hermes House, 1999.

Hartman'n Franz, M.D. *Principles of Astrological Geomancy: Art of Divining by Punctuation*. Boston: Occult Publishing Company, 1889. Reprinted, Mokelumne Hill, CA: Health Research, 1965.

Hopman, Ellen Evert. *Tree Medicine Tree Magic*. Custer, WA: Phoenix Publishing Inc., 1992.

Javary, Cyrille. *Understanding the I Ching*. Boston: Shambhala, 1997.

Jefferis, Alan and Madsen, David A. *Architectural Drafting and Design*. New York: Delmar Publishers Inc., 1986.

Kates, George N. *Chinese Household Furniture*. Harper and Brothers, 1948. Reprinted, New York: Dover Publications, 1962.

Kingston, Karen. *Clearing Your Clutter with Feng Shui*. Judy Piatkus (Publishers) Limited, 1998.

Kwok, Man–Ho and O'Brien, Joanne. *Elements of Feng Shui*. Dorset: Elements Books Limited, 1991.

Lau, Kwan. *Feng Shui for Today*. New York: Tengu Books, 1996.

———. *Secrets of Chinese Astrology*. Trumbull, CT: Tengu, Books, 1994.

Lau, Theodora. *The Handbook of Chinese Horoscopes*. New York: Harper & Row, 1979.

Linn, Denise. *Sacred Space*. New York: Ballantine Books, 1995.

Lip, Evelyn. *Chinese Geomancy: A Layman's Guide to Feng Shui*. Singapore: Times Books International, 1979.

———. *Chinese Numbers: Significance, Symbolism and Traditions*. Union City, CA: Heian International Inc., 1992.

———. *Chinese Practices and Beliefs*. Torrance, CA: Heian International Inc., 2000.

———. *Design & Feng Shui: Logos, Trademarks & Signboards*, Torrance, CA: Heian International Inc., 1995.

———. *Feng Shui for Business*, Union City, CA: Heian International Inc., 1990.

———. *Feng Shui for the Home*. Union City, CA: Heian International Inc.,1985.

Lippelt, Ulrich Wilhelm. *Feng Shui Demystified*. 1st Books Library, 2002.

Low, Albert. *Modern Living with Feng Shui*. Malaysia: Pelanduk Publications, 1998.

Marfori, Mark D. *Feng Shui: Discover Money, Health and Love*. Santa Monica, CA: Dragon Publishing, 1993.

Moore, Steve. *The Trigrams of Han*. England: Aquarian Press, 1989.

Paterson, Jacqueline Memory. *Tree Wisdom*. London: Thorsons, 1996.

Pennick, Nigel. *The Ancient Science of Geomancy*. Sebastopol, CA: CRCS Publications, 1979.

Post, Steven. *Modern Book of Feng Shui*. New York: Byron Preiss Books, 1998.

Roberts, Moss. *Chinese Fairy Tales & Fantasies*. New York: Pantheon Books, 1979.

Ronngren, Diane. *Sage & Smudge: The Ultimate Guide* Reno: ETC Publishing, 2003.

Ronngren, Diane. *Color: A Secret Language Revealed*. Reno: ETC Publishing, 1997.

Rossbach, Sarah. *Feng Shui: The Chinese Art of Placement*. London: Arkana, 1983.

———. *Interior Design with Feng Shui*. New York: Penguin Books, 1987.

Rossbach, Sarah and Yun, Lin. *Living Color*. New York: Kodansha International, 1994.

Sandifer, Jon. *Feng Shui Astrology*. New York: Ballantine Books, 1997.

Shêng–Han, Shih. *On "Fan Shêng–Chih Shu": An Agriculturist Book of China*. Written in the first century B.C.E. Reprinted, Peking, China: Science Press, 1974.

Simons, T. Raphael, *Feng Shui: Step by Step*. New York: Crown Trade Paperbacks, 1996.

Skinner, Stephen. *Flying Star Feng Shui*. Boston, MA: Tuttle Publishing, 2003.

———. *Living Earth Manual of Feng Shui*. London: Arkana, 1989.

——. *Oracle of Geomancy*. New York: Warner Destiny Books, 1977.

——. *Terrestrial Astrology: Divination by Geomancy*. London: Routledge & Kegan Paul, 1980.

Stellhorn, Donna, *Sage & Smudge: Secrets Of Clearing Your Personal Space* Reno: ETC Publishing, 1999

Stoddard, Alexandra. *Creating a Beautiful Home*. New York: Avon Books, 1992.

Sun, Ruth Q. *Asian Animal Zodiac*. New Jersey: Castle Books, 1974.

Swann, Peter. *Art of China, Korea and Japan*. New York: Frederick A. Praeger, 1963.

Tai, Sherman. *Principles of Feng Shui: An Illustrated Guide to Chinese Geomancy*. Singapore: Asiapac, 1998.

Too, Lillian. *Easy to Use Feng Shui: 168 Ways to Success*. London: Collins Brown Limited, 1999.

Twicken, David, Ph.D., L.Ac. *Classical Five Element Chinese Astrology Made Easy*. New York: Writers Club Press, 2000.

——. *Flying Star Feng Shui Made Easy*. New York: Writers Club Press, 2002.

Walters, Derek. *Chinese Astrology*. London: Watkins Publishing, 2002.

——. *Feng Shui: The Chinese Art of Designing a Harmonious Environment*. New York: Simon & Schuster, 1988.

——. *The Feng Shui Handbook*. London: Aquarian Press, 1991.

Webster, Richard. *Feng Shui for Apartment Living*. St Paul, MN: Llewellyn Publications, 1998.

Wilhelm, Richard. *The I Ching: Book of Changes*. Translated by Baynes, Cary. New Jersey: Princeton University Press, 1950.

Williams, C.A.S. *Outlines of Chinese Symbolism and Art Motives*. Shanghai: Kelly & Walsh Ltd., 1941. Reprinted, New York: Dover Publications, 1976.

Wing, R.L. *The I Ching Workbook*. New York: Doubleday, 1979.

Winston, Stephanie. *Stephanie Winston's Best Organizing Tips*. New York: Simon & Schuster, 1995.

Wydra, Nancilee. *Feng Shui: The Book of Cures*. Lincolnwood, IL: Contemporary Books, 1996.

Yoshikawa, Takashi. *Ki*. New York: St. Martin's Press, 1986. Reprinted as *Feng Shui Astrology*. York Beach, ME: Samuel Weiser, 1999.

Other References

10,000 Year Calendar (Wan Nian Li), Taiwan: National Publishers, 2002.

Concise English–Chinese, Chinese–English Dictionary. Hong Kong: Oxford University Press, 1999.

Lanbridge Pinyin Chinese–English Dictionary. Taiwan: Lanbridge Press, 1998.

Index

X

Y

In writing *Feng Shui Form*, Feng Shui Expert and Interior Designer Donna Stellhorn shares her more than 16 years' experience of problem-solving and working with individuals to improve their personal and business environments. Already a best-selling author, popular speaker, teacher and consultant, Donna is also an energetic entrepreneur who maintains a prize-winning Feng Shui wholesale and retail product line. She constantly strives to make both useful information and helpful tools available to all.

In her newest and most comprehensive book to date, Donna generously shares her experience and her expertise. *Feng Shui Form* is designed to offer both a broad basis of design and Feng Shui concepts as well as an informative and helpful compendium of useful remedies and cures so that we can instantly set about improving our own lives using the techniques and tools she so clearly defines.

Donna's childhood home in the Southern California city of Burbank was under near constant renovation as the family grew. This sparked her imagination and interest in home decorating and the importance of personal space. From a very young age Donna recognized the effects of a home's decor on the people who lived in it and their level of personal satisfaction. She determined to pursue a career that would allow her to work with personal environments and found answers to much of the puzzle of creating beautiful and harmonious personal spaces in the ancient techniques of Feng Shui as they applied to the concepts of interior design.

Following her studies in Los Angeles, in the early 1990's Donna moved to Albuquerque, New Mexico, the place that was to become her home for the next ten years. Her reputation as a Feng Shui Consultant grew as she wrote and published more than 80 articles on her favorite topic, lectured, taught classes and workshops and saw clients throughout the Southwest.

In 1995 she was invited to write her first Feng Shui book, *Fühl Dich wohl mit Feng Shui* for the European market. The book was published in 1996, introducing the concepts of Feng Shui and Interior Design to an eager readership overseas. During the New Mexico years Donna also started developing a product line of Feng Shui cures and began growing an online wholesale and retail marketplace.

Happily married to husband, Dannie, the opportunity came for them to move to Boston, Massachusetts in 2002. Now Donna successfully pursues the career that gives her an opportunity to share her concepts for enhancing comfort and good feelings by creating well-organized and harmonious personal environments. She communicates with people all over the world. Currently serving her community as the President of the Massachusetts Chapter of the International Feng Shui Guild, Donna Stellhorn also shares her insights via her workshops, speaking engagements, television and radio appearances, her writing and her personal consultations.

Donna Stellhorn's creative presentation of Feng Shui cures and products has brought her company recognition in the form of the First Prize, 2004 COVR Visionary Awards Winner for Home and Decorative Accessories. Her Feng Shui cures are sold in stores across the North American continent and in Europe.

To contact Donna Stellhorn call 800-918-2689

or visit her website at www.fengshuiform.com